Windmills, the River & Dust

OTHER TITLES BY JAMES C. WORK

Shane: The Critical Edition (1984)
Following Where the River Begins (1990)
Prose and Poetry of the American West (1991)
Gunfight! (1996)
Ride South to Purgatory (1999)
The Tobermory Manuscript (2000)
Ride West to Dawn (2001)
Ride to Banshee Cañon (2002)
The Dead Ride Alone (2003)
A Title to Murder (2004)
Riders of Deathwater Valley (2005)

Windmills, the River & Dust
ONE MAN'S WEST

James C. Work

Johnson Books • BOULDER

© 2006 James C. Work

All rights reserved. No part of this book may be reproduced or transmitted in any form or by any means, electronic or mechanical, including photocopy, recording, or any information storage and retrieval system, without permission in writing from the publisher.

Published by Johnson Books, a division of Big Earth Publishing,
3005 Center Green Drive, Suite 220, Boulder, Colorado 80301. www.johnsonbooks.com
email: books@bigearthpublishing.com

Cover Design by Polly Christensen
Cover Photograph by Branson Reynolds
Text Design by Erika Echols

9 8 7 6 5 4 3 2 1

Library of Congress Cataloging-in-Publication Data
Work, James C.
  Windmills, the river & dust: one man's West / James C. Work.
        p. cm.
  ISBN 1-55566-368-0
 1. Work, James C.—Homes and haunts—West (U.S.) 2. Authors, American—Homes and haunts—West (U.S.) 3. West (U.S.)—Description and travel. 4. West (U.S.)—Social life and customs. I. Title: Windmills, the river, and dust. II. Title.
  PS3573.06925
  [W56 2005]
  813'.54—dc22   2005017214

Printed in the United States of America

Contents

vii   PREFACE

1   *Windmills and Prairie*
3   **A WINDMILL ON THE PRAIRIE**

17   *The Farmer and the Bird*
19   **A CONVERGENCE OF CRANES**

29   *Of Time and Dust*
31   **FARMING THE DUST**

43   *Comes the Deer to My Singing*
45   **THE CHRISTMAS DEER DANCE AT TAOS PUEBLO**

57   *More Water, Fewer Mountains*
59   **IN SEARCH OF ESSENCE**

69   *Travels in the Mind*
71   **THE TERMINAL IMAGINATION**

91   **FOLLOWING WHERE THE RIVER BEGINS**

173   ENVOI

Preface

This book is dedicated to all the friends who wanted to see *Following Where the River Begins* back in print. I hope they won't mind my adding a few more essays.

As I sifted and sorted and arranged the material, I kept asking myself, "What do these essays have to do with each other? And with *Following Where the River Begins?*" The answer has something to do with values. Even more than a decade ago, while writing *Following*, I knew that I was weighing the value of individualism against the values of society. I was writing the story, but I was also trying to figure out our "proper" relationship with nature. Was it only a classroom, a museum, a writing lab? Or was it a refuge, a recreational facility, a place to "get away"? We know what nature has to offer us, but of what value are we to nature?

The "Epilogue" to *Following Where the River Begins* suggests that our values derive from three sources: our families, the society that gives us our education, and our active observation of our species. A grandfather tells us a story; a mother shows us the meaning of kindness; a teacher poses a question; or a chance encounter with a stranger leaves a long-lasting image in our mind. We call them "experiences," a word that in French means "tests" or "experiments."

If we remain alert to life, inquisitive and open, then each such experience is an opportunity to test the validity of our values. Simply pausing to think "what would my father do?" or "what will happen if I do this?" becomes the starting point of a personal experiment whose outcome we can guess at but can never predict absolutely. "I am a part of all that I have met," says Tennyson's Ulysses, "yet all experience is an arch where through gleams that untraveled world."

Somewhere in these essays I hope readers will find a doorway leading them back into their own past, or outward into some part of the world they have not yet imagined.

INTRODUCTION TO *A Windmill on the Prairie*

Windmills and Prairie

When I phoned Dad and told him about buying the windmill, I expected him to ask me why. When he was a boy back on the farm, it was a great day when they could afford an electric pump and let the windmill fall into disrepair. Having a windmill you no longer needed was a kind of rural status symbol.

"What did you get," Dad asked, "an Aeromotor or a Dempster?"

"Dempster," I said.

"We had an Aeromotor. I suppose Dempsters are alright. What kind of tower?"

"Well, right now I've got it mounted on a timber frame next to the porch. About five feet high."

"Oh. So it doesn't really do anything, then."

The iron machine with its long tail vane and six-foot wheel was the largest conversation piece in the neighborhood. Whenever we entertained, people would be drawn to it. I would watch them tentatively reach out and push one of the blades to see if the great wheel would turn.

"Does it work?"

"Sure. Well, it would if I dug a well under it. And had a pump cylinder."

Sometimes I'd get a wrench and take off the weather hood so they could peer inside at the gears and arms. Everyone had a windmill story. Either they had owned one, or had wanted to, or remembered one, or always wondered how the things work.

"What does it do? I mean, what do you want with it?"

"Mostly I talk to it," I would answer. "You wouldn't believe some of the things that old Dempster has heard."

I spent hours alone with it, listening to it hum and creak, taking it apart and putting it together again until I knew the function of every rod, cam, gear and bolt. When I had it all together and the wind took hold of the blades, it spoke to me as if all those metal parts had a soul.

As a youngster I took very little notice of the windmill on the farm. Like Grandfather, it seemed taller than life and unreachable as the sky. By all rights I should have attempted to climb the Fort Morgan windmill to look at it, for I was a boy of insatiable curiosity, like the elephant's child. And I loved any kind of machine. This one sat atop a high tower, but I'm sure it wasn't a fear of heights that kept me from scaling the Fort Morgan windmill. I climbed trees and cliffs galore. Back then, being the brainless lad I was, it didn't even occur to me to wonder *why* I had never climbed the windmill tower. But now I do wonder about it. I wonder if perhaps the tower was like Grandfather's life, far too remote, too dour and joyless for me ever to aspire to. Perhaps climbing the tower would create a certain bond between my life and his. Six days did he labor, my grandfather, and on the Sabbath he went to church to worship a God who seemed to me as distant and foreboding as himself.

I mounted my Dempster on a wooden stand next to the back porch where I could restore it and where I could get to know it on my own terms. When one of my grandchildren began trying to turn the sharp steel blades of the great wheel, I put it up on a tower.

A Windmill on the Prairie

It was the fresh and natural surface of the planet Earth, as it was made forever and ever. Talk of mysteries! Think of our life in nature—daily to be shown matter, to come in contact with it—rocks, trees, wind on our cheeks! The solid earth! The actual world! The common sense! Contact! Contact! Who are we? Where are we?

—Henry David Thoreau, "Ktaadn," *The Maine Woods*

One day I stopped along Highway 14 because I wanted to take a photograph of an old windmill. The brown, empty prairie at that spot made a particularly interesting background. A passing car slowed down and pulled off onto the shoulder ahead of my truck. The driver got out, thinking I was photographing a herd of antelope or something. We chatted awhile, agreeing that it was a nice day and a nice view and a nice windmill.

"Boy, oh boy!" he said, looking out across the windswept vastness of grass. "Wouldn'ya love t' own all this?"

"I guess so," I said.

"I'd like to have a windmill, too," he said. "Right in my backyard. Wouldn't that be somethin'?"

"It would be unusual," I said.

He had miles to go and things to do, so he got back into his car and drove away. But I lingered there awhile, just me and a meadowlark singing from a fence post. It was true, I thought. Almost everyone who sees an open prairie would like to own some of it, and most people probably would like to have a windmill to call their own.

He wasn't the first city dweller who has told me how much he'd love to have a few acres of rolling, open land. The same goes for farms and pastures. "Enough room to do whatever I want," another man once told me. "A place to grow something. Good place to raise kids." It's a natural feeling, at least out here west of the Ohio River. The wide-open spaces seem to provoke a kind of dim tribal memory of a time when actual contact with the earth was integral to life, a time not many generations ago when the westward-moving people "started out" to settle the frontier in Iowa, Kansas, Nebraska, Illinois and Missouri. A windmill is a kind of symbol of that, a machine that made prairie life possible. Now we live in houses where the only open space is a backyard where a fence shuts off our view of the neighbors. Our water comes from a tap.

But the guy who stopped along the highway and talked of owning a windmill and grassland will never buy himself that bit of prairie. To do so would mean giving up something else, such as the condo at the ski resort. It might cut into his retirement savings. Worse yet, he might not be able to sell it at a profit later on. In the meantime, what the heck would he *do* with a piece of prairie? He certainly wouldn't want to live on it, far from shopping malls and hospitals and schools. It would mean driving an extra hour or more to go skiing.

Same with a windmill. It would be great to own one and have it right there in the backyard. I know, because I have one. If he had one too, he could go out and release its brake and watch it spin whenever he wanted to. He could climb the tower. He might even get a permit to drill a small well, and then he could watch his own windmill pump water. Naturally that would mean he'd have to have the water tested and analyzed and approved, unless he wanted a lawsuit with the neighbor whose puppy got through his fence and drank his well water and got sick.

Then, too, if he lives close to shopping and hospitals and schools, there *will* be zoning laws and neighborhood covenants and liability insurance to consider. He'd be better off with one of those lawn ornaments that *look* like windmills and let it go at that. Even then the neighborhood association might not let him have it in his yard.

It's just as well, because prairies and windmills have one more thing in common: if you own either one of them, you'll need to spend some serious time with it. I don't mean maintenance, things like fixing fences and changing the gear oil. Maintenance takes time, but you can keep it to a minimum. When I say "spend some serious time," I mean the time you should spend just looking at the land and the machine and contemplating what you are seeing. It's a way of doing maintenance of the soul.

To really get in touch with your prairie, to understand what Thoreau meant when he said "Contact! Contact!" you need to take time to sit and consider all sorts of things you haven't thought of before. The depth of your prairie land, for instance. Not the acreage, but the *depth*. Let's imagine you are standing on a bit of prairie, a chunk of land. Just under your shoe soles there's a layer of soil of some kind, usually a tangled mat of plant roots feeding on decayed vegetation. Underneath this layer of soil there's probably a layer of sand and then maybe a layer of shale, and then a shelf of clay and finally, far down, bedrock.

I had a well drilled on my piece of the Colorado high plains. According to the driller's well log, the drill bit went down 297 feet and passed through twenty-two different layers ranging from a layer of rock that was five inches thick and a layer of blue shale five inches thick to a fifty-foot layer of mixed sand and shale. The drill even showed two layers of coal, one at 109 feet and one at 168 feet.

You can hire a geologist and a lawyer to tell you all about any mineral rights you might own, stuff you possess but will never set eyes on. It's all way down there out of sight. The layers of strata, hundreds or thousands of centuries in the making, are what determine whether your bit of land will slope to the west or to the east. When those layers decide to shift, they will cause the surface to heave and shake and make buildings fall over. If the world were an apple, geologists tell us, this skin of rock and shale and sand and soil would be about as thick as, well, the skin of the apple. Beyond that skin, far below the soles of your shoes, there's an ever-changing, ever-moving body of rock that goes all the way down to a molten core of magma.

It's almost too much for the human mind to grasp, so let's stand here with Thoreau's "wind on our cheeks" and contemplate the windmill instead. I didn't mention it to the man on Highway 14, but one reason I wanted a picture of that particular windmill was that it sat on a three-legged tower. Four-legged towers are more common. Wooden towers are pretty rare. If you want to figure out the height of a steel tower, count the girts. Those are the horizontal braces between the legs. They're usually between five and a half feet and six feet apart. A tower is only as high as it needs to be to catch the wind, so out on the flat prairie where trees are few you might see some that are only ten feet tall. In hill country where cottonwoods grow they need to be upwards of fifty or sixty feet.

That thing on top of the tower, looking like a car transmission, is what is called the "motor." On one end it has a big fan blade that knowledgeable persons call the "wheel." It will be anywhere from six to fourteen feet across. On the other end of the motor is the "vane," that long tail sticking out. Its job is to keep the wheel pointed into the wind. You can't see inside the motor unless you climb up there to the platform and remove the motor cover, but if you did you'd find a couple of gears, a couple of coupling arms and a lubrication system. Oh, and a brake of some kind. That's important, the brake.

The shaft comes out the bottom of the motor, drops down through the tower into the well and continues two hundred feet or maybe nine hundred feet down into the well. But notice something: the tower and the windmill are fabricated from iron, sheet metal and forged steel. There are only two places where wood is used, and it is crucial. Between the motor and the steel rod there's a length of wood. If the steel rod was connected directly to the motor, it could be too rigid and cause serious damage, so the wooden rod is there to take up the shock. It's called the "pump pole," if anyone ever asks you.

The other bit of wood is part of the tower. In fact, the bottom ground-level girts are made of wood rather than steel. Reason? Well, if one of the cows were to step on it, or if some mischievous kids jumped up and down on it, a steel girt would bend. And when it bent, it would tend to pull the tower legs together. Permanently. The wood will give and spring back. I think there's some kind of a lesson about life in there, somewhere, something about the need to stay resilient. Henry David Thoreau would know what that lesson is. But let's leave the tower and get on with our contemplation of the well.

Those who are not students of windmills and wells have never asked themselves where the pump is. After all, the whole point is to pump water. So where's the pump? You'll search for it in vain, because it is down at the bottom of the well, suspended at the end of a very long piece of pipe. The well rod, half an inch thick and made of steel or fiberglass, goes down through that long pipe to make the piston in the pump go up and down. Then the water rises up the pipe and out the spout. It's a simple little machine, this pump, nothing more than a steel cylinder with a piston in it, just like a hypodermic syringe with a one-way valve where the needle would be. The wheel turns atop the tower, the rod moves six or eight inches up, then six or eight inches down, and pretty soon water begins to surge up the pipe, out of darkness and into the glare of a prairie sun.

It gushes from the pipe one quart at a time or one gallon at a time, depending on the speed of the motor and the size of the piston cylinder. None of the machinery in the motor, none of the steel and wood and engineering that have gone into making the tower have any value whatsoever without that little syringe-like cylinder, the tube and piston working forever unseen down in the darkness of the well.

A windmill is a collection of parts, an assemblage of metal. Its sheet metal was forged and welded and riveted into vanes and blades. Its cast metal was formed into the shapes of cams, Pitman arms and eccentric wheels. Machined steel became shafts and pins and bearings, swivels, brakes, sucker rods, sheaves, pivots, springs and pullouts. Each piece was designed and fabricated separately, but it all comes together for a single purpose, a single function. It is made to draw water out of the earth and up to the surface—where it will, in a few days or in a multiplicity of eons, find its way down again to the aquifer.

But that's about enough on windmills and wells. Let's sit back against the tower and feel the thrumming vibration while we turn our thoughts to our piece of prairie.

Like the windmill, a prairie is an assemblage of parts and materials. It is made of cells, atoms, molecules, chemicals and energy in the shape of plants, animals, insects, soil, rocks, people, roads, fences, floods, tornadoes, hailstorms, sunshine, darkness and birdsongs. Whether animal, vegetable or mineral, each particle of this prairie began as a microscopic nothing. Each atom merged miraculously with others to become something larger, something with a function to perform in the life of the land, moving forward on the scale of time only to return eventually to dust and then to atoms again, back to the source.

This is what is so time-consuming about a prairie, the contemplation of it all. Making a thorough study of a square foot of it, even a square inch of it, could occupy you for a lifetime. First you make contact ("!"), then you begin to mull over how the parts make contact with one another. What does this ant have to do with that antelope? How did this flake of obsidian come to lie next to a grain of basalt? This is why a windmill and a bit of prairie can be so time-consuming, once one begins to contemplate the connections. And the *meaning* of the connections.

I have frequently seen a poet withdraw, having enjoyed the most valuable part of a farm, while the crusty farmer supposed that he had got

a few wild apples only. Why, the owner does not know it for many years when a poet has put his farm in rhyme, the most admirable kind of invisible fence, has fairly impounded it, milked it, skimmed it, and got all the cream, and left the farmer only the skimmed milk.
    —Henry David Thoreau, "Where I Lived," *Walden*

Back on Highway 14 while I was enjoying the sunshine and thinking about the three-legged windmill, I was skimming the best part of that acreage. Even while standing there I was already beginning to write about it. It goes further than just writing about it, too. What we like to call the "ownership" of a piece of land has almost nothing to do with scraps of legal paper called deeds and titles. True ownership, ownership of the essence, goes to whoever is willing to invest time in contemplation.

☙

A number of years ago, I inherited eighty acres of prairie. It is typical of the high plains in that it is made up of rounded hills, gentle dips and valleys, and a couple of sudden steep-walled arroyos. Less typically, it features a dozen or more stands of ponderosa pine ranging from fingerlings to a few old-timers over sixty feet high. The land is rich in yucca and bluestem grass, wildflowers and antelope tracks. When the breeze is blowing the trees seem to be humming softly. The first time I camped on this land it seemed complete and perfect for relaxation and contemplation, except for one thing. What it needed, I decided, was a water tank. I arranged for a man to drive out from the nearest town and begin drilling a well. In the meantime, I went shopping for a windmill I could afford.

The "*Used Windmill, Fair Condition*" listed in the classified ad turned out to be a pile of junk that showed dim signs of having once been a 1930 Dempster Model 12. The old rancher who wanted to sell it told me he had used a tractor to drag it from one well to another until it got too old and bent up to be worth the trouble. Cheap electricity and efficient electric pumps had arrived on his ranch, so he relegated the Dempster to the scrap pile.

It was lying in a heap with other discarded machinery, hardly recognizable as a windmill motor and wheel. Weeds grew up through the warped blades. The vane arm was bent nearly double. The draw rod was bent into a J shape. It looked hopeless. But I had driven quite a few miles to see it, so I decided to clear away some of the junk and get a good look. The

A Windmill on the Prairie

rancher wandered off to see if he could persuade his old Ford tractor to run—"just in case you want to load the windmill into your truck"—while I pulled on my gloves and began to dig down through the tangle of rusty wire and hunks of rotten plank. Following one of the crushed blades down to the wheel spider, then uncovering the main shaft, I moved old pipes, old fence posts, unidentifiable remains of various farm machines, until I had excavated the motor.

I loosened the single bolt holding the weather hood and lifted it off to look inside.

Most of those abandoned windmills you see when you drive the back roads in farming country were abandoned because of a crack in the motor casing. Sometimes, it got cracked because the tower fell down, or was pulled down, and the impact broke the cast iron. Sometimes, water gets into the gearbox and freezes and cracks the metal. And sometimes, people with hunting rifles shoot holes in them. Then the oil leaks out, the gears go dry and seize up, and the motor is ruined.

I looked into the grease-caked gearbox. I cleared away some more junk and turned it over. The cast-iron casing was intact. Not a crack, not a bullet hole. The motor would hold oil. Better still, the irreplaceable Pitman arms were still in working condition, and so was the main shaft. The Dempster Model 12 could be brought back to life.

Rebuilding it took more than a year, and whenever I wasn't hammering the blades and vane back into shape or scouring ancient grease out of the gearbox, I was searching for a suitable tower. I found one at a farm auction, and I got it cheap. There were two reasons for that. First, the people at the auction were looking for "collectibles" and things to decorate their suburban half-acre plots. They were willing to pay a hundred dollars for a worn-out wheelbarrow or walking cultivator. One lady paid fifty bucks for a leaky cream can and a cracked brown jug. But nobody seemed to want a three-legged, sixty-foot tower in their yard.

The second reason the tower came cheap was urban expansion and city "development." The farm was scheduled to become a shopping mall and the old tower was in the way. According to the auction catalog, it was "to be removed by buyer, before January 20." I paid the auctioneer and then started to wonder what I had let myself in for. Imagine looking up at a sixty-foot steel tower, with your little crescent wrench in hand, wondering where to begin.

I began by hiring a man with a mobile crane. While I applied my wrench to the half-inch bolts, he kept it from falling over. After nine corroded bolts and a bit of inventive cursing, we lifted the whole structure off its supports and laid it down. Then I proceeded to take it apart a bolt at a time, a strut wire at a time, a girt and section at a time. On a very cold and bitter January day I dug six feet into the ground to retrieve the three leg anchors, heavy six-foot lengths of angle iron with wide feet at the bottom. Each one meant that I had to dig a hole six feet deep, two feet wide, and six feet long. In January.

While I was out there slamming the digging bar up and down, over and over just to gain another inch of loose dirt for the shovel, I thought about my pioneer ancestors who homestead on the eastern Colorado plains. They had to do the same labor. They, too, had to dig deep holes for anchor footings to put up their own windmills. They had to manhandle sixty-foot sections of steel into place. They had to cobble together a jury-rigged kind of derrick arrangement atop the tower in order to hoist the two hundred–pound motor. And once the motor had been hoisted into place and the tower centered over the well hole, they had to get the wheel to the top of the tower and slide it onto the motor shaft. Then they lowered the pump, screwing sections of pipe and draw rod together (without dropping them down the hole) until finally all the parts and pieces were in place. If it all worked correctly, and if the wind blew, a surge of water would come pouring out of the pipe.

By digging deep wells and setting up windmills, that first generation of prairie farmers and their wives made a compact with the Great Plains. "Here we are," they said, "and here we will stay." With towers and windmills they anchored themselves to the land. That man who stopped to see why I was taking a picture of a windmill, the man who said he would like to own "all this" never will own it because he does not want to be anchored to it.

~

Today's farm homes have electric motors and ingenious submersible pumps. Whether there is wind or no wind, the electric pumps push a steady supply of water up to a pressure tank and the pressure tank causes it to come out the kitchen tap at a constant rate of flow. Someone turns the tap and the water starts to flow. It works so well and is so dependable that it is taken for granted.

But imagine what it would be like to look out the window to see if there will be wind so the livestock will have water to drink, or if there will be enough to do the laundry. I can imagine my grandmother doing that. I can imagine my grandfather squinting into the sun to see which way the vane was moving. The direction of the wind told him what kind of weather to expect. Sometimes he must have watched the vane slowly swinging the blades this way and that way as if it was smelling the light afternoon breeze for water. Once or twice a year he climbed up sixty feet of narrow metal ladder to grease the steel gears or change the oil, maybe pausing to gaze windward, wondering if there would be enough wind, enough water.

I have never had to pay much attention to the source of my water. I just turn the tap. But I know that in doing it I have lost a connection to "the actual world."

That's enough about faucets. Let's talk about wind instead. More specifically, about wind and fragility. On the prairie, wind is the movement of life. Seeds drift on the wind. Windblown fires purify and fertilize the soil. Soil moves on the wind. The wind turns the windmill, but too much wind can whirl a windmill to pieces. Ever since the first ones were invented, and all through the centuries of windmill engineering, there has been that one problem. How to cope with too much wind.

Some patented windmills incorporate governors to regulate the speed of the wheel. Others, like my Dempster Model 12, have a thick wire running down one leg of the tower. When that wire is pulled, the tail vane swings over until it is snugged up against the wheel. In that position it keeps the edge of the wheel into the wind. If the wheel were allowed to point directly into a heavy wind, it would fly apart. Turned sideways, it can survive a gale.

Fire invigorates the grassland. Century upon century, fires swept the prairies. Trees could not survive these infernos, nor could any invasive species of plant. But the grass survived. The grass burned down to its strong roots, fed upon the nitrogen in the ash and char, and came back even greener and stronger than before. Like the windmill turning sideways to the gale, the grass let the fire sweep by and came back the next spring stronger than ever.

Sometimes we need to do that, too.

But much depends on balance. When sleet covers the windmill wheel it accumulates on the tips of the downward blades. If it is caked with ice when the wind comes along, it can wreck the whole machine. A few pounds of thick fog frozen into a thin coating on half the blades, or just one blade, will throw the whole thing out of balance. The turning wheel

A Windmill on the Prairie

starts to lunge. The lunging motion is like a hammer banging away at the Pitman arms and the driveshaft until something snaps.

It's like having some small fear build up on one side of your brain and having your thoughts go round and round until they worry you half to death.

Far down in the darkness of the well, deep under the motor and tower, the pump cylinder knows nothing about sleet or fire or roots. It just responds to the rise and fall of the sucker rod, sending its little quart or two of water to the surface. If everything up top is kept in good balance, the pump will keep the water coming.

❧

But to get back to our discussion of the prairie, I would like you to point to the stars for me. Put down the book and point at the stars.

Which direction did you point?

Nearly every person you ask to do this will point in one direction: straight up into the sky. Almost none will realize they need to point in every direction instead, all around, upwards and downwards. The stars are everywhere around our Earth. Nietzsche wrote, "As long as you still feel the stars as being something 'over' you, you still lack the eye of the man of knowledge."

Nietzsche knew what he was talking about.

Go onto the prairie at night, somewhere beyond any glimpse of any light created by humans, and try pointing at the stars. Try to choose a piece of prairie where the earth spreads away from you in every direction, where you can see the Earth's curvature in the horizon. There, if you try to point at the stars, you will find yourself with both arms spread wide and your head tilted back, staring open-mouthed into the depths of space.

Nietzsche also wrote, "when you gaze long into an abyss, the abyss also gazes into you." He was saying that we may begin to feel the *anima* of the stars and sky and prairie as if it were reflecting our own life-spirit back to us. We may sense a sort of transfer taking place, an exchange between ourselves and open space. It takes strength and patience and endurance to stand and calmly stay still and look long into the prairie, but if we *do* stay long enough and look long enough, we will find the prairie looking back into us. "Look again," wrote Samuel Scudder in his essay on becoming a scientist. "Look again! Look again!"

If you find yourself fortunate enough to be in the proximity of a real working windmill, you may be tempted to climb the tower. And if you do, you'll discover a few things about perspective. First, the ladder is so narrow that you can barely put both feet on the same rung. After you have climbed partway, the tiredness in your arms will remind you how steep it is. When you finally reach the platform, you'll find that it's rather difficult to haul yourself up onto it. My Aunt Charlotte became a family legend at age three when she climbed to the top of the farm's fifty-foot windmill tower. She also found that the wider perspective it gave her came with a price, for Grandfather was a dour old Presbyterian Scot with no time to waste in rescuing little girls who should know better. "She found her way up," he grumbled to Grandmother, "and she can find her way down again."

One would think one could see the prairie better, standing on a windmill platform clinging to the motor. But there are better places to choose. From that narrow platform it is a long drop to earth, and the tower seems unusually fragile. It seems as if it were going to start swaying at any moment, as if it couldn't sustain the weight of a human. You might have climbed up there for the view, but once there you'd like nothing more than to be down on the ground again. Like most of our machinery—cars, computers, televisions—the windmill tower *separates* us from earth. The difference is that we have become so used to cars and computers and televisions, the distance they impose between ourselves and the earth no longer frightens us. We don't even sense that there *is* a distance.

Luther Standing Bear wrote, "The Lakota was a true naturist—a lover of nature. He loved the earth and all things of the earth, the attachment growing with age. The old people came literally to love the soil and they sat or reclined on the ground with a feeling of being close to a mothering power . . . for to sit or lie upon the ground is to be able to think more deeply and to feel more keenly; he can see more clearly into the mysteries of life and come closer in kinship to other lives about him . . . he knew that man's heart away from nature becomes hard."

I rarely write poems. But one evening after the Dempster 12 was up and running, I found myself overcome by a desire to write about it. I was standing next to the tower, making contact with the steadily thrumming metal as the windmill spun in a light breeze high above. I remembered it as I had first seen it, a pile of grease-encrusted junk. I remembered the first time I put my hand out to touch it.

While touching twisted vanes, and probing mummifying grease
For fatal fractures of the casing, I wondered:
Who else has touched these remnants of wreckage,
These rusting artifacts of the prairie covenant between machine and prairie?

The metal replied:
"My vanes touched the wind. All and any wind, I embraced it.
Beneath my tower, I touched earth. Through my casing and my shaft
I was intimate with strata, shale and sand and stone,
Clay layering loam layering clay again;
And water I touched, ancient water squeezing
Through midnight rock.
I touched sky . . . I touched sky even on days
When unshaded sun-scorch made the vanes and blades
As blistering to the skin as forge-fresh steel;
On days when adamantine frost froze into
Galvanized scales so cold as to weld mittens to the
Metal (as well as unbelieving tongues of boys).
Sometimes the ice made my brittle blades labor,
My gears grinding through frozen oil.
I also touched human hearts on certain nights, on certain
Moving air nights, slicing the melon moon in my blades
And making stars wink on and off
With my iambic of pump rod and piston."

Back to the well. The well is a very narrow cylinder a little larger in circumference than a coffee can. It is a long shaft of total darkness beneath the windmill tower, leading down to the piston that sends the water up. It goes straight down through sod, clay, shale, rock; through old riverbeds; through skulls of mammoths and through lacy fossils of prehistoric flowers; through ancient seashells. Imagine the slender rod those hundreds of feet of pipe contain, silently rising and falling past countless generations of life now layered like a deck of cards. Think what a textbook it would make if we could ourselves descend that vertical shaft of time! We would first see the fresh leaves on the surface, last year's mulch beneath that, and finally the fossil leaves down at the last layer.

Were you to ask a paleontologist how deep the prairie is, she might tell you it is as deep as the lowest fossils are found, meaning that in human terms the prairie's depth ends where organic life began on the planet. Were you to ask the same question of an agronomist, he might say the prairie is defined by the depth of accessible topsoil. Anything deeper than that has little relevance because we can neither move it nor plant things in it.

Ask a geometry teacher. The geometrician might suggest the surveyor's platted and plotted square of prairie actually extends downward in the shape of an inverted pyramid, a theoretical model coming to a point at the exact center of the globe. But then you may ask why it could not be thought of as continuing on from there, ascending in another pyramid to the other side. Perhaps any prairie worth its sod goes clear through the planet.

Or ask an astronomer. If you have chosen your astronomer well, the answer may come in the form of two arms extended upward and outward. The arms mark another pyramid, or perhaps a cone, leading upward. It diverges and extends infinitely, beyond the far margins of our own universe, up through all the stars, on to the very edge of creation. For somewhere out there beyond the reach of any of our machines or even our imagination there may *still* be found a speck of prairie.

Stand in front of the next windmill you come across. Imagine the deep shaft running down into the fossilized past beneath your boot soles. Think of the winter storms of ice and wind that windmill survived merely by turning sideways to the force of it. Contemplate water. Sketch the pattern where the vertical lines of well and tower intersect the horizontal prairie horizon.

Think of Thoreau, but not the Thoreau who lived in a tiny cabin by a small lake in the woods because, as he said, he wanted to drive life into a corner. I mean the Thoreau who stood on the top of Mount Ktaadn.

It was the fresh and natural surface of the planet Earth as it was made forever and ever. . . . Talk of mysteries! Think of our life in nature— daily to be shown matter, to come in contact with it—rocks, trees, wind on our cheeks! The solid earth! The actual world! The common sense! Contact! Contact! Who are we? Where are we?

☙

INTRODUCTION TO *A Convergence of Cranes*

The Farmer and the Bird

This next essay is about looking up and looking down, being aware of the sky and the earth at the same time, seeing the Big Pattern while you take care of the temporary details. What each part does for the whole, you might say, like the components of a windmill.

A windmill is a great thing to look up at. If you're really lucky enough, you can sit with your back to a tower leg and feel the thrumming of the turning wheel coming through the ground. But even if you're not on a first-name basis with a windmill, you still need to spend a few minutes of each day just gazing upward. Look up a tree or a flagpole, anything taller than yourself.

Whenever you raise your eyes high enough to see over the people who hurry along sidewalks, there is always the chance that you'll see some birds in flight. Just a few speeding sparrows or a wayward wren, maybe, or a whole flock of Canada geese or a patrol of crows. There's something strangely fascinating about birds flying, the way a formation of pigeons suddenly wheels in the sky with a silver flash of many wings, or the way a soaring hawk hangs motionless on the wind.

This essay is also about farming. Who can drive past a field being plowed without slowing down to watch? Who hasn't stopped to gaze and gaze across fields of wheat or corn that seem to roll endlessly on like soft swells of the ocean? I love to be in cafés or hardware stores, coffee shops or county fairs, wherever I can hear farm people talking. There's poetry in their language. Stan Smith was a man who knew that poetry well; he and I would drive back roads in central Nebraska and talk about it for hours. Poetry, and birds. And farming.

"Look at that," Stan might say. "Herman Novak's got his combine going. Probably start harvesting the milo this week."

"Maybe."

"Do you know that poem by Don Welch?"

"About cutting milo? Yes. What's it called? 'Lines for My Father'?"

"That's the one," said Stan. And then, "Dry work, farming is."

"True," I might answer. "So is reciting poetry. Dry work, I mean."

"A man should take precautions."

"Right."

That was our signal. If it was morning, we'd head for a place that had coffee. If it was afternoon, we knew of certain blue-collar and overall taverns where a man could take more malty measures to prevent dying of thirst. But only if there were no cranes to be seen. If there were sandhill cranes on the farm fields along the Platte, we'd both risk drought and dehydration just to lean on the fences and watch them. The cranes of Nebraska look exotic, oriental, magical. Like the Platte, they are unlike any other bird you've ever seen. I have canoed the Niobrara, the Dismal, the Loup and the Republican Rivers in Nebraska, and there is no water like the water of the Platte. And no farmers such as you find there.

A Convergence of Cranes

> *O the one life within us and abroad,*
> *Which meets all motion and becomes its soul,*
> *A light in sound, a sound-like power in light,*
> *Rhythm in all thought, and joyance everywhere—*
> *Methinks, it should have been impossible*
> *Not to love all things in a world so filled.*
> —Samuel Taylor Coleridge, "The Eolian Harp" (1795)

You don't see many "Eolian harps" these days, but back in Coleridge's time they were all the rage. People hung them in their gardens and put them in their windows or wherever a breeze might blow across the strings, much as we use wind chimes today. An Eolian harp was little more than a rectangular wooden box with a dozen gut strings stretched over it. The wind harp's strings were tuned to the harmonics of a single tone so it would hum different chords as the breeze changed in intensity, playing an infinite variety of haunting sounds and never the same one twice. The motion of the wind and the vibrations of the strings became sounds that left "rhythm" and "joyance" in their wake. Wood and gut converged with wind, and music was born.

"One life, all motion, rhythm in all thought." But what does it mean? I'm going to venture out onto the proverbial limb here and suggest that people who work in buildings are going to read Coleridge's blank verse differently from people with outdoor jobs. Indoor workers will interpret the phrase "one life . . . all motion" to refer to *routine*. The daily grind. The weekly schedule. A routine project. Being hired, getting paid, being retired—the same old schtick, the same old rhythm of life.

People with outdoor jobs will be more likely to read "one life" to mean *change*. Change in the seasons. Change in the weather. There's a change in the air. Time to change tools, change clothes, change chores. Looks like winter's coming. Sure hope this means that spring's on the way. The rhythm of life. The rhythms *in* life. Life in the rhythms. A life of letting the winds strum your harp for you.

∼

"How many damn cranes do you people *need?*" the farmer asked my friend, there beside the Platte in the middle of Nebraska on a bitter March morning.

My friend was Stan Smith, one of "those people" who watch birds. Stan was also an unofficial census-taker of wild bees, a walker of rivers, watchman of corn tassels and monitor of clouds. Every week Stan would sit down at his typewriter and write me a letter about how things were going in his river valley. He would report on whether the goldfinches had turned yellow, whether the feral cats had kittens, and how the three-legged fox was doing. Stan would write to tell me when it was time for the farmers to burn their ditches, in case I wanted to come help watch the prairie raptors diving on rodents as they ran out of the flaming weeds.

Stan's Platte runs through central Nebraska. Here in Colorado, my Platte has two parts. Both branches—the North and the South—begin high up in Colorado's subalpine zone. Up there where alluvial meadows are terraced by centuries of beaver colonies, the sky is mirrored in a myriad of ponds that shine like polished glass. The beaver ponds gather the snowmelt, gently releasing the water into hundreds of quiet little creeks. The creeks join forces, picking up speed and becoming a single rushing river that leaves the meadows and goes tumbling down through rocky gorges where it erodes the granite boulders, undercuts the steep talus slopes, and pours through chasms too deep for the sun to penetrate.

Late one October, at the upstream end of a dark chasm, I stood hip-boot deep in the North Platte trying my luck at late-season flycasting. Snowflakes drifted down through the gray sky. The water was so clear I had no trouble seeing my #18 Hornberg floating out at the end of its 2x leader, a tiny speck of lint on a long strand of hair. The river was low, since last winter's snowpack had finished melting a month before, yet the moving water still had the power to drag at my legs. When I turned into the wind to make a cast, I was looking at the mountains where the Platte is born. How could those mountains, large as they are, manage to store up so much water? How could a river with so much muscle keep flowing all summer long and with scarcely undiminished strength?

The river current raked gravel from under my feet. I braced myself to finish a cast, stiffening my back against the tug of the water and the gusting wind. A trout came up off the bottom, made a false pass at my Hornberg, and went down again. It was a beautiful fish and the last one I was going to see that season. Soon the snow would fill up the high valleys, the bugs would stop hatching, the fish would stop biting, and I would stop trying. Until next spring. That's the rhythm of the sport.

The next spring did indeed find me on the Platte River again, but in the middle of Nebraska. I had a book in mind, something about how river confluences are metaphors for life. I had been to the junctions of most of the Platte's tributaries, such as the Cache la Poudre River, and I had gone to where the Platte joins the Missouri, and now it was time to find a place to sit and contemplate the confluence of the two Plattes.

Cold wind plastered my jacket against me and pelted my face and hands with flying sand. The sky was slate. The two branches of the river were flowing full, but silently; so noiselessly did they slip through the sandhill bluffs that I could hear the hum of traffic on Interstate 80, a mile to the south. A dozen gulls rested voiceless on the Y-shaped sandbar made by the merging rivers. Franklin's gulls, I guessed. Too early in the season for herring gulls to show up, but I'd visit Stan on my way home and make sure. He'd know.

The cold morning quiet was made deeper by the distant highway undertone and by the whisper of wind among the bare willow and cottonwood branches. The two rivers met and married with perfect calm, there on the prairie; mild swirls and miniature ripples gave little evidence of the deep turbulence taking place under the broad surface. Drawn up on a sandbank nearby were two dredges and four barge-shaped pontoons quietly going about the business of rusting away.

It was right here at the confluence, in 1939, that engineers threw a dam across the river and constructed heavy gates and locks to divert the married waters into a new, artificial bed. It's called the Tri-County Supply Canal. Here the mountain-born Plattes cease to be rivers and become an irrigation canal.

The canal is impressive; I'll say that for it. Fifty feet wide, banks lined with stone—which had to be imported, since Nebraska rock is pretty scarce—the Tri-County has sufficient capacity to divert the entire Platte River. And it *does:* downstream of the diversion structure, the riverbed is

A Convergence of Cranes

only dry sand showing a thin, faint stain of moisture that has seeped under the dam.

So what were these two rivers, before they merged and became the Tri-County Canal?

Well: after leaving its high mountain valleys and rampaging down its granite gorge, the North Platte leaves Colorado and enters Wyoming. A hundred miles into Wyoming it hits a dam and becomes Seminoe Reservoir. Soon after that it fills the Pathfinder Reservoir. Reaching Casper next, it turns southeast toward the Nebraska panhandle. But first it has to supply Wyoming's Glendo Reservoir with water. From Glendo it moves out onto the high plains and into Nebraska, where Kingsley Dam blocks its path to form Lake McConaughy. After McConaughy is satisfied, the North Platte is free to flow on through wheat fields and sand hills toward the confluence.

Like the North Platte, the South Platte is also born of melting snow-packs above timberline in Colorado. In the mountains west of Fairplay, in tundra basins eleven thousand feet above sea level, the fledgling Platte trickles through moss and glacial sand. The trickles join to become creeks, then streams, and then a river.

Eleven Mile Canyon Reservoir makes the first impoundment of the South Platte. Then South Platte water goes to Cheesman Lake, then Chatfield Reservoir. Once these two have satisfied their thirst, Cheesman and Chatfield let the river go. It makes a run through the city of Denver, goes north to Greeley, then swings west again. Just past the town of North Platte, Nebraska, it joins the North Platte.

Once out of the Rocky Mountains and into the flatlands, the two branches of the river saturate shallow aquifers that fill countless gravel pits and ponds where people picnic and swim and fish for crappie, bluegill, bass and catfish. Wells dug into the aquifer irrigate lawns and crops. Dredges scoop up Platte sand and gravel for the making of concrete. People drift on the river in boats and inner tubes, deer drink from it, and raccoons wade it looking for crawdads.

And for two months each spring the spreading shallow ribbons of the Platte become a vital safety zone for the migrating sandhill cranes.

~

"How many damn cranes do you people *need?*" asked the farmer.

~

The convergence of sandhill cranes and the Platte River is predestined, part of a rhythm that begins even as the embryonic bird is still inside the egg. It begins even before that: embryonic cells containing microscopic memory bytes already hold genetic information about what the Platte looks like and how to get there. It is as if at the moment of your conception when that one certain sperm cell touched that one certain egg, it was already providing you with a map to lead you back to where your parents were born, and their parents, and all the parents before them.

The crane egg drops into the world in late May, landing softly and safely in a nest resembling a big pile of grass clippings. The heap of grass and moss most often sits on frozen or spring-soggy tundra, near open water, somewhere along the Yukon Territory's swampy coastal plains, or further north on Alaska's shores. Some of the nests are across the Bering Sea, in Siberia. But whether a bird is born in the Yukon, Alaska or Siberia, the rhythm of life for the crane chick will be the same, year after century after millennium. It begins when the chick hatches. It goes on into a brief arctic summer, during which the chick feeds ravenously and grows at incredible speed.

By the time September blizzards start to sweep across the tundra, the young birds must be big enough and strong enough to migrate south. Joining along the way with other flocks coming in from Saskatchewan, Manitoba, Alberta, they form into enormous sky-filling squadrons of gray phantoms leaving the Arctic Circle to fly down the wind. They pass over Canada; they overfly Montana or the Dakotas; they cross Nebraska at eight thousand feet and keep on flying, over Kansas, over Oklahoma. By the time they finally glide down to earth to rest, they are either on the Rio Grande or the Pecos River in New Mexico, or in the Muleshoe Refuge of west Texas.

Throughout the winter, there in the warm bosques and ciénagas of the Southwest, the cranes feed and gain strength. On the nearby fields, they dance their courtship dances and those who are old enough for mating form lifelong pairings. Mating takes place, eggs start to form, and in the fertilized cells, the crane's ancient knowledge of the Platte is passed on to the next generation of birds.

In March, the cranes leave the warm fields and river bottoms and retrace their route, flying back north to their arctic birthplaces. But there is a difference between this long journey and the one that brought them south: now they must fly into the prevailing winds, burning energy at a frightening rate. For the survival of their species it is imperative that they stop to rest and find nourishment on the Platte River. If their eggs are to be strong enough to survive the next laying, if the giant birds are to have the strength to fly from the Rio Grande to the Arctic with those eggs, they *must* pause at the Platte valley. No other place will do. For six weeks they will spend their days in the farm fields, consuming leftover grain, weed seeds, insect larvae and worms. They will spend their nights roosting where they will be safe from predators, on the shallow sandbars in the Platte.

I should say "roosting by the thousands." The Big Bend Audubon Society of Kearney estimates that 500,000 cranes use the central Platte as their staging area. Morning and evening during that six weeks people come from miles away just to stand and watch the spectacle of a half million gray birds making wheeling, turning patterns in the sky.

≈

Let's go back for a moment to the mountain headwaters of the Platte. These cliffs and peaks were born during a Rocky Mountain uplift that took place 28 million years ago. In a book titled *Sandhill Cranes: Wings over the Platte,* the Nebraska Game and Parks Commission notes that "fossil evidence indicates that the sandhill crane has been a part of Nebraska's fauna for at least the last 10 million years."

Up until the agricultural tribes of Europe arrived about two centuries ago, the Great Plains were all grass. Almost no trees. Summer lightning started prairie fires that burned off any trees or bushes that may have started to grow, and those same fires enriched the soil for the next generation of grass. In spite of wildfires, trees and brush still might have forested the banks of the river were it not for the fact that the Platte flooded each spring. It spread out for miles across the valley, washing out everything but the toughly rooted grass. In those days the river was made up of wide, shallow veins in a braided network twenty miles wide and three hundred miles long. There was water and grass and little else. When Francisco Vásquez de Coronado ventured onto the Great Plains in his 1540 expedition, one of his officers wrote that the grass of the Great Plains was as tall as his saddlehorn and extended unbroken from horizon to horizon. With no trees and no landmarks, soldiers made cairns of bison bones and dry manure so they could find their way back to Santa Fe. They had never seen such a treeless expanse. Even their language had no name for it.

A Convergence of Cranes

For millions of years before Coronado and for four and a half centuries afterward, the cranes have landed on the same prairie to consume dry seeds and insects by day and to seek the safety of the open, shallow river by night.

Coronado went away, not having found his cities of gold, and the plains and the cranes were left alone along with the Native Americans. But then, beginning with the Mallet brothers in 1739, a steadily growing stream of trappers, hunters, soldiers, traders and explorers encountered the Platte—"the Nebraska seacoast." By 1860, farmers had begun digging ditches to get Platte River water to their fields.

In 1939, two hundred years after the Mallets "found" the Platte, the confluence diversion structure was built. In the dry riverbed downstream of that dam, blowing sand whips at tall cottonwoods and willow where once ran the Platte. Agriculture needs the water, and takes it. Further downstream, the surplus "return flow" is put back into the riverbed, but it is only a small fraction of what was taken out.

Until the irrigators came, the cranes had the river to themselves each spring. After fighting the high-altitude winds without rest all the way from Texas, they would spot the dark twisting ribbons of water far ahead just as their genetic memory said they would. Coasting down by the hundreds of thousands, thousands of waves of birds kept landing for hours. As night fell they sought the sanctuary of the Platte's shoals and islands. At daybreak they rose from the river and flew to the prairie grassland—now the grain fields—where they would feed and dance and rest. They could count on it. It had been this way forever.

The humans who dammed and diverted the river made it possible for prairie cottonwoods and sandhill willows to grow on the sandbars. They also put an end to uncontrolled grassland wildfires, encouraging uncontrolled forestation. The forests and trees helped keep the Platte to a single channel and eliminated most of the shallow sandbar flats where the cranes once found safety.

Seventy years of irrigation. Only seventy years, just one human lifetime, and the cranes are restricted to one narrow band where the Platte still runs in many ankle-deep rivulets through unforested sand. The Nebraska Game and Parks Commission estimates that 70 percent of the remaining sandhill cranes are confined to 80 miles of river—60 miles between Lexington and Grand Island, 20 miles between North Platte and Sutherland.

☙

I stood on the bridge at Gibbon, Nebraska, one evening in March, waiting for the cranes to come to their night roosts on the river. The sun was down. The light was failing. Someone shouted "Here they come!" and we saw them. Hundreds of streamlined forms against the twilight, gliding over the cottonwoods. "Here they come!" someone else said in a few minutes, and here came another flight. Another. And more and more. For two hours, flight after flight of cranes came.

I watched the strip of river upstream where the cranes were going to land. Twilight made it look like a metallic mirror reflecting the night sky. I focused my binoculars on one particular section and saw the river becoming blacker and blacker until a solid island of dark extended from bank to bank and up- and downriver. They were cranes, blanketing the shallows. Chirring to each other, calling, preening, settling down. Two hours of gray phantoms flying low and landing, filling up the entire river from bank to bank.

With each new group of birds, whether it was six or sixty, someone would point into the dark steel sky and say to the rest of us, "Here they come." How many did we need, that evening?

&

I imagine the pioneer farmers who settled along this river also must have stood in awe, leaning on their shovels in the thawing days of March, watching a million wings filling the heavens as flocks of cranes drifted riverward, coming out of the sky like downward streamers of smoke.

For a hundred and sixty years, the Platte valley farmer has watched the cranes arrive. While he wonders if it is safe to plant, the cranes clean the old weed and wheat seeds from his fields; they turn the stubble and the mulch; they aerate and manure the soil; they devour tons of insects and insect larvae. And at night they go to the river.

Unlike the sandhill cranes, the farmer does not migrate. He is rooted to the land. At the same time the cranes feel the ancient urge to fly north, the farmer is starting his own spring rhythm. He watches the mail for seed catalogs. He visits equipment dealers. He is in town more often, drinking coffee with other farmers. He drives more slowly on the back roads, watching for new green shoots in the fields.

The cranes cruise at 6,000 feet or higher, watching the same land for signs of spring. In March the wind at that height blows cold from the north and west. They search for the shining silver ribbons far below their wings, thin ribbons that reflect the sky in lines and loops and curves all tangled through the prairie. The water. The place they must rest.

The farmer feels the cold wind drying his sweat. He has been fixing a piece of equipment, since he has no spare cash for a new one this year, and he doesn't need any more debt just now. Maybe with a good crop, plenty of water, good harvest weather, and if prices stay up. Maybe.

The cranes. "How many damn cranes do you people *need?*" Whatever the number, it will affect the amount of irrigation water he can have for his crops. He wipes his hands on an oil rag and watches the sky as he listens to the voices of the ancient ones, the gray ghosts.

The cranes. Landing, they are already covering the field. Family groups of three or four are calling to each other, staying in touch. Some cranes are already doing their mating dance and others are feeding. Some are exhausted and simply stand or lie down with their heads laid back along their shoulders, sleeping.

The cranes do whatever they please. They know no bankers; they go from Siberia to Mexico and never pay any taxes anywhere. They take their living from the earth and from the water. They mate for life; they raise their young and never have to buy them clothes or send them to school. They sleep on the sandbars of the rivers, safe, without title or mortgage.

They owe nothing and own nothing but the prairie skies. The farmer owns the fence his foot is resting on and everything inside that fence. He grows food for thousands of others, while the cranes give people nothing. Even so, there are these people who want to take the farmer's water and spread it out on the dried-up riverbed for the birds. All the cranes will do is stand in it while they watch it run away, unused, to the Missouri.

~

When harvest is over and autumn comes to the fields, the cranes will be flying back from the Arctic to Texas. They will not stop at the Platte, but the farmer might happen to be looking up one day and see them, scores of long V's soaring silently down the cold blue sky at great heights. He may hear their distant cry as it floats down like a faint sound from a faraway Eolian harp. The birds have nested and raised their young and are taking the youngsters south once more.

The farmer has had his water and his crop for another season. He has seen the birds going over and he knows they will return again, as surely as the sunrise will move a little more south on the horizon each day. It's one of those rhythms of life.

One of these days, the Platte irrigation controversy, the Great Water Issue, is going to come down to a question of farmers versus cranes. As long as there is some shallow water on the Platte sandbars, and as long as farmers' fields supply seeds and insects, the cranes will return to central Nebraska.

Maybe the farmer will move to a greener and less arid region, but I don't think so. I think he will stay in the Platte River valley so long as the cranes keep on returning. He will stay there so long as he can look up and see them coming down the sky with the March sun on their breasts and the early spring wind beneath their wings. He will always look up when they call, and he will know the season.

How many cranes do we need? Well, it depends upon where you are standing, and how many you want to count.

INTRODUCTION TO *Farming the Dust*

Of Time and Dust

> And Time, a maniac scattering dust,
> And Life, a Fury slinging flame.
> —Alfred, Lord Tennyson,
> *In Memoriam,* Stanza 2

Lord Tennyson never saw eastern Colorado, but Time certainly scattered a lot of dust there. Our hope-filled pioneer farmers optimistically called it "soil." They had their Fury-driven flames, too, when the lightning came without rain and set the grass afire.

I have two images in mind. The first is a memory I have of flying back across eastern Colorado after a trip to England and Scotland. Seen from the air, the British Isles were a patchwork of green forests, green lawns and green fields. Over New England and the terrain lying east of the Missouri I looked down on even more green prairies and forested hills. When the plane began its descent into Denver, I saw nothing except shades of tan and brown with a few patches here and there of thin green.

"It's been a drought year," I apologized to the passenger across the aisle. "We usually get about twelve inches of rain a year. Last year it came on August 4."

My second memory is of seeing a farmer kneeling in a dry field, crumbling a clump of dirt between his fingers. From the dust that remained in his palm he took some seeds and saw that they were dead. They had put out no roots. They had no future. Three generations earlier his forefathers had arrived on these very same fields with no roots and little future. His legacy was two quarter-sections of powdery dry topsoil.

When Dad married Mom, they moved away from the family farm at Fort Morgan. They bought a place on Fall River near Estes Park, five acres with seven small cabins, two outhouses and a central shower. Dad began to add frills and extras, such as wallboard to cover the bare stud walls and enameled tin cabinets in place of the dynamite boxes that served as cupboards.

At first they called their enterprise a "cabin camp," then "motel." Mom always hoped it would someday evolve into a "lodge," but I'm not convinced they bought it with that idea in mind. I think they bought it because of the river. And the well. A water-witcher told Dad there was an underground stream beneath Workshire and it ran straight into the well. The idea fascinated me. We not only had a real river, with all the small trout and slippery rocks and dangerous rapids a boy could want, but our own underground river too! Sometimes Dad opened the well to repair the pump and I would be there to peer down into the musty darkness, wishing I could see that underground river going past.

As a boy, I assumed they had bought the place for me. I had trees to climb, mountains to wander and a river for skipping rocks and catching trout. But there was more to the decision than that. Last summer I went in search of Great-Grandfather Josiah's river out in eastern Colorado. In the 1890s he and some other newly transplanted easterners formed a company to take irrigation water from Bijou Creek. I found the "Bijou" part soon enough, a regular jewel of a riverbed meandering through the farmlands. But I didn't see any "creek" to it. The creek part is sand. It could be called the Bijou Sand Dunes or maybe the Sahara Bijou. Still, full of faith that rains would come to fill that channel of silt with water, Josiah Work and his partners hitched heavy teams to scrapers and Fresnos and built themselves a reservoir. They sold shares of the water they imagined would someday arrive. They constructed a ditch system to take it from the reservoir to the farms.

Today, a hundred years into their future, it's all sand. The fields are dust. And my father took his bride to live on a crystalline river running down from the timeless snows of the mountains.

Farming the Dust

I heard this story years ago:

A little girl found her mother reading. "Mommy," she asked, "is it true that people are dust before they're born and after they die?"

"Yes, dear," the mother replied. "The minister tells us we go from dust to dust."

"Then you'd better look in my room," the girl said. "Somebody's either coming or going under my bed."

There's another story in which a little boy asks his father where he came from and after a long agonizing attempt at explaining bird and bee biology, the father gives up and asks his son what it was that prompted the question. "Tommy says he came from Milwaukee," the boy said, "so I wanted to know where I came from."

Following the publication of Dr. Bryan Sykes's book *The Seven Daughters of Eve* in 2001, so many people wanted to explore where their DNA had come from that a web site was established to deal with the interest. Even those who don't need to know the source of their DNA still find their cultural heritage fascinating. Are they part Greek, Spanish, Irish, Norwegian? If Great-Great-Grandfather came over from Italy, does that explain why they like lasagna? Does the family tree include Native Americans? Do family members have a tartan, or maybe a coat of arms? How about a link to Russian nobility?

The literary epic is all about cultural identity. Homer wrote *The Iliad* and *The Odyssey* to help the Greeks remember who they were. The same goes for the Spanish who saw their ancestors in *El Cid,* and the French who make their kids read *The Song of Roland.* Even Milton's classic *Paradise Lost* was written to teach Christians about their origin—and their downfall—in the Garden of Eden.

One of my favorite American books is N. Scott Momaday's *The Way to Rainy Mountain.* It's a slim, quick little volume that captures the very essence of the Kiowa people's concept of themselves as a culture, verbalizing, as Momaday puts it, "who they were" and the "traditions of [their] reality."

N. Scott Momaday is one of those western kids who grew up Indian in a cowboy world. However, he was never confused about his cultural identity. His Kiowa relatives made sure of that, especially his grandmother. She knew exactly who she was, just as she knew exactly who the Kiowa are. After finishing graduate school and becoming a professor, Momaday set out to follow the odyssey of the Kiowa as they made a migration that took centuries to complete, all the way from the northern Rockies to Rainy Mountain, Oklahoma. He gathered up fragments of stories, shards of memories, bits of dimly remembered experience. To these he added his remembrances of his own growing-up time, making personal contact with "the living memory and the verbal tradition" of the Kiowa.

Teaching *The Way to Rainy Mountain,* I became so interested in Momaday's unique approach to writing a cultural record that I began to sort out my own personal and cultural memories. And as I began to separate my memories into three categories—things I knew I had actually experienced, things I only had been told about, and things I had been *told* I had experienced—some unexpected questions popped up. For instance, my grandfather Work was a farmer and my grandfather Hays was a salesman. So where did I get my addiction to words? How did I end up being a lover of language and literature? As early as seventh grade I was collecting what I thought were wonderful examples of poetic writing, most of which I taped inside my school locker. None of my chums did that. If they had anything taped inside their lockers, it was pictures of football heroes or John Wayne wearing a marine uniform. Lots of my buddies had "funny" last names, but I seemed to be the only one who wanted to know where mine came from. At a time when my best friend didn't even know his grandmother's maiden name, I knew that Grandmother Work's was "Stewart." More than that, I learned that this royal name originated with the ancient term "sty ward," which originally referred to keepers of the swine pens and later came to refer to any kind of personal servant or steward.

Wherefore was I first among the sixth graders to learn what "wherefore" meant? And wherefore, years afterward, did I become a teacher of literature? These were the kinds of questions stirred up by *The Way to Rainy Mountain*. The book inspired me to revisit dimly remembered scenes of my childhood, and I began to see that those memories contained keys to my self-meaning. It is very easy to identify with the tribal customs and beliefs of my people; I love to watch the Scottish dancers and hear the bagpipes at annual highland festivals. I love to look at hills of heather and foggy lochs, but they do little or nothing to tell me what it really means to be descended from the people who left the highlands and made the long, long migration to the plains of eastern Colorado.

My ancestors, dubbed the "Scots" by the Romans and Anglos who invaded their islands, were a northern tribe. During times of war they painted their faces. In prehistoric times they lived in dark, remote mountains before making a centuries-long migration down into the open midlands. Then came foreigners who spoke in strange tongues and who gradually, relentlessly deprived them of their Celtic language, their oral history, their hereditary lands and their religion. Seen from this perspective the Kiowa and the Scots would seem to have much in common.

As the centuries slowly passed, the conglomerate of invading foreigners became known collectively as "the English," very much like disparate batches of Europeans later became called "Americans." The English forced the Scots to migrate across the Irish Sea and into the nine northern counties of Ireland, where they would be called "Ulstermen."

Speaking of words and language and culture and such, should Dr. Momaday refer to himself as "Indian," "Native American," "Kiowa" or *Kwuda*? By the same token, should I call myself American, Scot, Scotch, Scotch-Irish or Ulsterman? People who attend highland festivals will argue hotly for one term or the other. But it is no longer important enough to go to battle over. What remains important are the culture's basic traits, behavior and ideology.

English economy and English greed created a need for cheap labor in the New Land. So Ulster folk, desperate for some way to make any kind of living, were recruited to work in the American colonies. Now they would be known as "Americans" or "colonists" as well as Irish-Americans and Scotch-Irish. In the language of prejudice they were shanty Irish, Micks and jocks. In America they discovered how to earn title to a piece of land with the sweat of their brows and in quick order, they built farming communities up and down the Atlantic coast from Virginia to Nova

Farming the Dust

Scotia. More and more arrived, heading west across the mountains. Carrying a Holy Bible written by God, Moses and John Knox, the people whose warriors once painted their faces and went to war wearing kilts eventually arrived on the western prairies where they were to pit their legendary stubbornness against the tough, unyielding earth.

To tribes such as the Kiowa, the Scotch-Irish were the foreigners who spoke in strange tongues. The invaders gave the Native Americans new names, forced them into a position where they would either have to fight to the death, migrate to unknown lands or submit to confinement on "reservations." Second-class citizens in England and Ireland, it was now the Scots' turn to deprive Indians of their religion, make them learn a new language, and generally treat them like second-class human beings.

☙

In *The Way to Rainy Mountain* the sacred Tai Me and the holy grandmother bundle are central images of Momaday's recollections of his grandmother and the house in which she lived. I find it wonderfully ironic that Momaday, a formidable-looking male descended from warriors and dog soldiers, spends time writing about his female ancestor. Instead of telling stories of men battling the enemy, of male sacrifice and heroic action, Momaday finishes his book with images of his honored grandmother. It is ironic but not surprising, for by the end of his narrative he has returned to contemplating the essential source of life, the force that shaped his cultural past. That force is, in the words of Frank Waters, the "female imperative."

I, too, am a descendant of a race that revels in tales of men facing hopeless odds and making heroic sacrifices, not with lances and bows but with the dirk and claymore and broadsword. There is much excitement in those legends of Robert the Bruce and Rob Roy. But finally, as Momaday well knows, a person's cultural inheritance includes something of far more importance than legends of warriors. The prime force, the essential "what is" of any story of the Kiowa or the Scots or any other culture you care to name can be found in the annals of Eve's descendants, not in accounts of battle and victory but in the grandmother chronicles.

THE COMING OUT

Momaday: "The great adventure of the Kiowas was a going forth into the heart of the continent."

Farming the Dust

The Kiowas came one by one into the world through a hollow log . . . there was a woman whose body was swollen up with child, and she got stuck in the log. After that, no one could get through, and that is why the Kiowas are a small tribe. They called themselves Kwuda, *'coming out.'*

It is a legend fraught with implications and mysteries. *Why* did the *Kwuda* ancestors suddenly decide to go away from their familiar mountains? Why, once they had started, did they create the legend about going from a dark place into a place of sunlight, and why through a hollow log? And why did they say it was a female who was to blame for the tribe being divided into those who went away and those who had to remain?

It was also a female, you remember, who ate the apple. The Second Book of Genesis says: "To Adam the Lord God said 'because thou has eaten of the Tree of the Knowledge of Good and Evil, cursed is the ground . . . in the sweat of thy face shalt thou eat bread, till thou return unto the ground; for out of it was thou taken: for dust thou art and unto dust shalt thou return." (Even the language of King James was regarded as the only true language of worship.)

As I learned the story, at my Scottish Presbyterian grandmother's knee, so to speak, we Protestants interpret Genesis as meaning that woman was not *only* to blame for the loss of Eden, but because of her transgression she is forevermore required to be subservient to man as well as to God. We men, we noble and self-sacrificing creatures, left Eden for her sake, and now we all have to work like hell to stay alive. When we die, supposedly, Hell is *still* an option, but the choice isn't ours. All because of Eve and that accursed apple. What was she *thinking,* listening to a snake in the grass?

༄

Mary Elizabeth Stewart, the first of five children of the Reverend Albert Struthers Stewart and his wife, Charlotte E. Campbell, grew up full of intellectual promise. She had that love of words that the Scots value so highly. She was valedictorian at Wooster High School in Wooster, Ohio; graduated from Indiana Normal School in Indiana, Pennsylvania, in 1899; and taught school for two years before marrying James Ewing Work. Her honeymoon was a train ride from Newburgh, New York, all the way to the almost treeless plains of eastern Colorado. The train ran on coal, which sent rancid smoke and cinders back along the cars. The windows were open because of the stifling heat and tobacco smoke. Mary Elizabeth would have worn a proper corset and sundry undergarments beneath her long heavy skirt. Hour after hour after hour, sitting on hard seats in stiff clothing, she could pass the time by having conversations with James, by watching the prairie go endlessly by, or by reading.

I think she read. James was probably busy making plans and discussing economics and religion with two of his brothers, whom he had brought along on the honeymoon. The three of them were to join their father Josiah and become dryland farmers.

Mary Elizabeth had grown up on quiet, tree-shaded streets in Pennsylvania and New York. James Ewing brought her to a three-room house that sat in the middle of an empty prairie. He was an idyllic young easterner with no knowledge of farming except what he had read in books. In his luggage were a few government pamphlets describing how to raise profitable crops without irrigation. His distant ancestors probably raised sheep and cattle in the highlands, but his grandfather and father were loggers and lumbermen in Pennsylvania. James now built a barn, got himself a team and plow, and set out to make a living from the land as a beet farmer. Meanwhile, Mary Elizabeth stored food in a dirt cellar; hauled water and boiled it on a woodstove to wash clothes; fed and butchered chickens; baked bread, carried food and water to fieldworkers; churned butter; fought constant dust with feather duster, broom and carpet beater; and bore five children of whom four reached adulthood.

In her spare time, she read books.

GOING ON

Momaday describes a storm cellar at his grandmother's house. "There are many of those crude shelters in that part of the world," he writes. "They conform to the shape of the land and are scarcely remarkable: low earthen mounds with heavy wooden trapdoors that appear to open upon the underworld."

The cellar entrance at the James Ewing Work farm was a gaping, dark rectangular hole in the concrete floor of their screened back porch. When you opened the squeaking screen door on its patented self-closing hinges, the cellar hole was immediately to your right next to the kitchen door. You had to walk around it in order to get to the kitchen. To this day I can close my eyes and still see that forbidding hole in the floor and the rough concrete steps leading down into the dark. Steep and uneven, they were steps that wouldn't meet building code standards for a badger burrow. The "safety railing," a single splintery, sagging two-by-four nailed to a pair of posts, would give a child welfare agent fainting apoplexy.

The rectangular opening looked like nothing so much as an unfilled grave. At the bottom of the stairs was a door of wooden planks. I remember carefully descending the steps, one hand against the wall to keep my balance, then lifting the latch and pushing the door open. Out came a wave of odors—the clean smell of dirt, the dustier smell of potatoes and turnips. A barrel of apples—the forbidden fruit of Eden—gave off the most tempting scent of all, tangy and sweet. Crude wooden shelves held jars of preserves slowly gathering dust. No, wait: "slowly" isn't accurate. In the dryland farm atmosphere of eastern Colorado, those jars acquired a coating of dust the day they went onto the shelves.

With the thick door open and the single hanging lightbulb turned on, I could see a wooden rocking chair standing next to the butter churn. At Grandmother's funeral, a neighbor said it was common to find Mary sitting down there in the light of that one bare bulb, one hand moving the dasher up and down while the other held an open book. My mother told me Grandmother Work was able to read a book while cooking, knitting, even while ironing. And did. When she caught a ride into town with someone—she never learned to drive a car—the unspoken arrangement was that Grandfather or one of her children would pick her up later at the library. She would always end up at the library.

I can picture her now, coming through the squeaking, banging screen door into the cooler shade of the earth-scented back porch, a carpetbag of library books on her arm, walking around the open cellar, hanging her town hat on its peg, and then going into the kitchen to start supper. As she put the crank handle into the front of the cookstove to shake down the clinkers, or as she lifted the lid to replenish the fire with kindling, she must have thought wistfully of the cool, quiet cellar. The cellar, her second-best rocking chair, and a new book from the library. It was a great deal to look forward to; I know, because I am her grandson.

ᴥ

Mary Elizabeth Stewart grew up in New York, sheltered from the sun by forests and serenaded by streams. Our ancient Scots ancestors—hers and mine—also lived in glens where deep rich forests thrived. But politics and industry brought that world to an end. First came the genocidal era of Cromwell and Charles the Second, years that Scots still refer to as the "Killing Times." After the Killing Times, the "removals" started. As soon as the hereditary owners of those glens had been removed, the hardwood forests were cut down and hauled away to become the hulls of British ships and fuel for British foundries. The logged-over highlands became pasturage for hundreds of thousands of sheep owned by wealthy absentee landlords. Now the old highlanders were in the way once again.

Scotsman Hardy W. Campbell was the chief advocate of dryland farming methods on the treeless "wastes" of the American prairie. James Ewing Work and others read Campbell's pamphlets and followed his instructions. Dryland farming was the newest agricultural technology, the only way to reclaim the desert and make the barren land bloom, the way to turn nothingness into God's garden. Of little interest was the ancient sod except for building temporary houses, or the tall grass except to be twisted into fire fuel, or the dwindling bison except as target practice.

Campbell's dryland farming method called for heavy teams of horses or oxen and steel plows that were considered massive in their time. The plows penetrated deep into the earth to break up subsurface loam and increase its ability to hold moisture, forming a kind of subterranean reservoir. After each rain, farmers rushed out to plow again, turning the earth between rows of crops in an attempt to get the precious moisture down to the roots before it could evaporate. During dry days, of which there were plenty, they used harrows to pulverize dry topsoil into silt and pack it down in hard layers to retard evaporation. It was called "dust mulch."

The problem with dust mulch is wind. Eastern Colorado is frequently swept by a wind that is born somewhere north of Saskatchewan. Migrating southward, it loses moisture over Montana, stops off for a quick beer in Cheyenne, then comes howling across the Platte River like a banshee with two hernias. Instead of carrying moisture, it carries dirt. The Book of Genesis tells that, after the unfortunate episode in Eden, Jehovah condemned the serpent to eat dust all the days of its life. In eastern Colorado, the same thing went for humans.

Between battles with silt that continually drifted over her windowsills and under her door, Mary Stewart Work planted seedling trees and watered them with buckets of wash water or fresh water she drew from the well. Fresh or full of greasy soapsuds, it all came from the well, not from a tap. Sometimes in the Dust Bowl days, she went out to find drifts of fine dirt completely covering her tiny trees. But she kept digging them out, watering them, and protecting them with old fruit baskets and scraps of corrugated tin, and by the time she died, her front yard was walled in with tall cottonwood, ash, maple, elm, pine and spruce trees. Her personal forest still didn't make the farm look like New York State, but at least it softened the view of the plains. When my father took the family to visit his parents, it meant driving all the way from the mountains to Fort Morgan, a distance of nearly a hundred miles. My brother and I would stand on the backseat of Dad's 1948 Buick as we rolled east along Highway 34, each of us trying to be the first to see the farm. Suddenly we'd spot the windmill, then the roof of the barn, and then the trees.

In back of the house, Mary grew gardens of berries, potatoes, onions, corn and cucumbers. Wild rabbits and feral cats lived in the juniper hedge, along with squirrels and birds. It was a refuge, a sanctuary from the brutal wind and merciless sun, and she and James Ewing created it in just one lifetime. Not so long ago I stood beside her grave and silently wondered why. Why did she work so hard, out here in the Great American Desert? Was it to reclaim the highlands or reconstruct her verdant New York surroundings there in far-off Colorado? Was it religious stubbornness? What is there in Scots that drives them to do battle with hard surroundings? I think I understand why Josiah and James Ewing went a-pioneering to far-off Colorado. But what was Mary Stewart doing there?

Maybe, down deep in her Protestant-taught subconscious, she was doing her part to redeem Eve.

~

"Bad women are thrown away," Momaday writes. His book tells the story of a man who went blind and had to rely upon his wife to tell him where to point his arrow, that they might have buffalo meat. Three times she told the husband that his arrow had missed the mark, when it had not; then she took all the meat and her child and ran away, leaving him alone to starve. She told the people he had been killed by enemies. But the truth came out when the blind man returned to the camp.

"That was a bad woman. At sunrise they threw her away."

No one remembers Mary Stewart ever complaining when James launched one of his hapless projects, such as the time he set out to raise popcorn. Popcorn, he was told, brought twice as much money as field corn. The problem, he discovered, was that the Fort Morgan Grain and Elevator Company couldn't sell so much as a gunnysack full of popcorn, let alone five tons of the stuff. Livestock wouldn't eat it. Making matters even worse, popcorn cross-pollinated with field corn and ruined most of it.

Mary Stewart listened with love and sympathy as James bewailed the cost of the seed and the time lost in the labor. Then she swept her house and sat down with a book.

James Ewing had a sister who did beautiful calligraphy. She gave Mary a large handmade wall poster, framed in glass, and for as long as I can remember it hung in the dining room above her chair. It showed a family saying grace before eating the dinner set before them, and underneath was inscribed Robert Burns's "Selkirk Grace":

> *Some hae meat and canna eat,*
> *And some wad eat that lack it;*
> *But we hae meat and we can eat,*
> *And say the Lord be thanket.*

At the Presbyterian Church, which James helped build in Fort Morgan (just as his father, Josiah, built the church at Brush), Mary Stewart held the congregational record for Sabbath School attendance. She was never absent. On the rare occasions when she was out of town, she attended Sunday school wherever she was and brought back a note to prove it.

CLOSING IN

Momaday closes his book with a description of a woman who was buried wearing a beautiful dress. "It was one of those fine buckskin dresses, and it was decorated with elk's teeth and beadwork. That dress is still there, under the ground."

Paul, in the First Epistle to Timothy, said "let women adorn themselves in modest apparel, with shamefastness and sobriety; let a woman learn in quietness with subjection; permit not a woman to teach, nor to have dominion over a man, but to be in quietness."

But Mary Stewart did teach school, as did all the Work women I ever knew or heard of. Three aunts, Ruth and Elizabeth and Janet, taught in the Fort Morgan schools all their lives. Stern, serious spinsters, these three never suffered a fool at all, let alone gladly. When I began teaching at Colorado State University, I could identify Fort Morgan kids the moment I announced my name was Work. Some turned pale; some just looked as though they might turn and flee.

"You're from Fort Morgan, right?"
"Right. I had a teacher there and her name was Work, too."
"And how did you like her?" I would ask.
"Well . . . I learned a lot, I guess."

One photograph of Mary Stewart shows a room so cluttered with furniture that it almost looks like it was intended to be an inventory of the parlor and that she is in it by accident. She sits in profile like Whistler's mother, off to one side of the picture, her back stiffly straight. Her head is slightly bent over the book she is holding open in one hand. I wonder if she paid someone to take it. Maybe she used her "egg money" to pay for a picture to send home to the family in New York, so they'd know she and James had prospered enough to afford a furnished parlor.

Maybe, while the photographer was setting up his tripod and camera and getting his flash powder ready, Mary Stewart picked up a book—or what is more likely, took one from her apron pocket—and soon she was so lost in the words she was unaware of what he was doing. Unaware too, for the moment, of the vast plains encircling her small house, her struggling garden, her storm cellar.

෴

When one of the spinster teachers, my aunt Janet, died a few years ago, I brought home some of her books. Among them I found two beautifully bound volumes of Tennyson inscribed in a fine feminine hand "Mary E. R. Stewart, July 1900."

The date is three years before her marriage. The Tennyson volumes were probably a graduation present given to her as she went off to begin teaching. Looking inside I found dainty checkmarks beside certain titles in the table of contents. And when I looked at those poems I found certain stanzas underlined. One such stanza is from Tennyson's "The Palace of Art":

> *I built my soul a lordly pleasure-house,*
> *Wherein at ease for aye to dwell,*
> *I said, "O Soul, make merry and carouse,*
> *Dear soul, for all is well."*

She also had underscored, in light pencil, two lines of "In Memoriam":

> *Our wills are ours, we know not how;*
> *Our wills are ours, to make them Thine.*

In "Idylls of the King" grandmother had marked these lines:

> *Break not, O woman's-heart, but still endure;*
> *Break not, for thou art Royal, but endure.*

Grandfather spent most of his days outside in the dust of his six hundred and forty acres. Grandmother spent most of hers inside her small house and, as much as was possible, in the pages of her books. To her the word was everything.

"In the beginning," according to the Gospel of John, "was the Word."

I have stood in Grandfather's fields at dusk with the smell of earth in my nostrils and thought how much it would mean to a sixteenth-century highlander to be owner of such vast acres. I have thrilled to the falling tremolo sound of a nighthawk and the sharp sudden bark of a fox. I have stood with a shovel, the blade of good steel and the handle of stout ash, and looked away to glorious horizons. The double-bit axe of the Pennsylvania Works is something I'm well acquainted with.

I have also entered the pages of books; countless times I have lost the world among the words. If I had to choose which to leave to my children and grandchildren, had to choose among leaving them land, a tradition of honest toil or this strange affection I have for squiggles on a page, it would be the squiggles. In the words I found my soul, my essence, my spirit.

Momaday calls the journey of the Kiowa an evocation of three things: a landscape that is incomparable, a time that is gone forever, and the human spirit, which endures. His people and mine, the spirit of the culture enduring. Through our grandmothers, through the stories, enduring.

INTRODUCTION TO *The Christmas Deer Dance at Taos Pueblo*

Comes the Deer to My Singing
—from a Navaho hunting song

Deer came frequently to our house, their heart-shaped tracks on the dirt road becoming circumstantial evidence about who had been browsing Mother's pansies and nasturtiums. I knew deer, but I was unaware that such things as deer dances and deer ceremonies even existed. I did know, however, the ritual of fishing. At first light I slipped out the kitchen door and closed it quietly. With the silent mountain morning listening, I gathered up my fishing rod, canvas creel and a Prince Albert tobacco can full of fresh worms. My thin arms shivered inside my jeans jacket as I made my stealthy way through the dew-wet grass down to the river.

After long ice-locked months of winter, May had finally arrived, the month that would bring about the Last Day of School and the Opening Day of Fishing Season. I began volunteering to do chores for pocket money until I had enough for my first visit of the season to one of my personal shrines, National Park Outfitters. They had racks of guns smelling of Hoppe's #9 bore cleaner, a display case of dangerous knives, and shelves bearing the weight of canvas tents in boxes, but most importantly they had fishing stuff. After sufficient deliberation, I solemnly picked out my purchases and put my money on the counter.

"Here you go," Mr. Fonda said. "Two packets of snelled Eagle Claw hooks and one tin of split shot."

If I had a quarter left over, I'd buy a bottle of salmon eggs.

"Good luck," Mr. Fonda said.

"Thanks," I replied, with all the gravity of a big-game hunter about to enter the bush in search of rhino.

On the night before Opening Day I checked my equipment and stashed it just outside the back door. I made promises to my mother that I would return bearing trout, that tomorrow's supper was all taken care of. Being a very wise mother, she would forgo her usual warning to be careful. One does not warn hunters to be careful. And when morning finally arrived, I was gone from the house before sunrise and wading through wet grass, eager to get to the one certain place on the river where I always made my first cast.

It was the nearest thing to a ritual I knew. There was meaning in it, but I did not know that. The meaning was not in the morning, or in the preparations. Nor was the meaning in me. It was in the trout and in the search for the trout. And even after I realized that, years after, I didn't know what the meaning was until I read *The Man Who Killed the Deer.*

The Christmas Deer Dance at Taos Pueblo

Long ago, according to the legend, men and animals lived together and understood each other.
—Erna Ferguson, *The Dancing Gods*, 1931

They all gave way before her.

The wild deer and graceful antelope, the massive buffalo, the wily coyotes, the snarling wildcats and mountain lions, and all the fawns and cubs. They all drew back shudderingly, with strange low sounds, from the sacred, inviolable Deer Mother. And when after a time she turned, eyes down as if unconscious of their presence, they followed her in great circles, spirals and diagonal lines of dancers. Followed her in the soft, powdery snow, uttering their strange low cries of resentment, their snarls of defiance, but unable to resist and being led back again into a long oval.

Within it the drum kept beating.
—Frank Waters, *The Man Who Killed the Deer*, 1942

The drum draws the spectators down the narrow passage between adobe walls past the mud-plastered church. It pulls people into the open plaza where they look nervously about for a place to stand and not be noticed. The insistent beat makes conversation seem awkward, trivial, invasive. Most people stand waiting in silence, not knowing what is about to happen. They know there is a heavy-bellied deep-voiced drum beating somewhere nearby, sending a steady rhythm of vibration through the air and through the ground. They catch occasional glimpses of men carrying animal costumes. The mountain behind the pueblo walls seems to be listening. It is waiting for the Deer Mothers to appear, and the men dressed as animals.

Erna Ferguson saw the ceremonial in the 1920s and described it in her book, *The Dancing Gods*. She is accurate in every detail and has the ethnologist's knack of separating the elemental from the incidental. But I found her description of the dance too remote, too much as if she had written it after her soul had forgotten the sound of the drums. Frank Waters, on the other hand, makes the Deer Dance into an episode of wonder. There was never any danger of Frank forgetting what the drums sound like: his adobe house stands at the very edge of the pueblo.

For centuries the pueblo of Taos has occupied the center of a flat plain surrounded by mountains. It is seven thousand feet above the level of the sea and forested with piñon, cedar and sage. The Sangre de Cristo mountains loom up over one edge of the plain; in the opposite direction the plateau comes to a sudden end at the deep gorge of the Rio Grande.

Calendar photographers and people who produce tourist brochures see Taos Pueblo as little more than a photo opportunity. Thanks to travel magazines, it is probably the most recognizable Native American habitation in America. Photos generally show the large open plaza with the little mountain stream running through it, as well as the two five-story adobe buildings facing each other. They are made of square rooms stacked like pyramids of soft brown building blocks. Each one of these is a house with a family. Each one has its small window and painted door. Wooden staircases and wooden ladders lead up to the higher levels. In bright daylight, you can see curtains at the windows, chimney pipes, stacks of firewood and drying racks. But at sunrise or dusk these kinds of details fade to invisibility. The texture and color of the adobe walls also fade, and in the hours between deepest dark and new morning sun, the high mud buildings look like two ancient, immutable mesas facing each other across a timeless stream.

~

Christmas Day was cold that year. The sky was cloudless turquoise. A layer of ice covered the little stream, except for occasional openings where the water ran swiftly. Soft snow covered the ice, covered the rooftops, and blanketed the ground. Eighteen inches of snow had fallen just before Christmas, and because the weather had been so cold and so dry, it was still pure white, crisp and clean, without puddles of snowmelt, without mud.

The pueblo had plowed and shoveled the plaza for the dance, leaving high piles of packed snow that made ideal vantage points for those of us who had come to watch the ceremony.

My wife and I and our two friends stood on one of these hard snow piles close to a log footbridge that spanned the stream. We shivered and hugged our coats around our bodies. We stamped our feet to keep our toes from going numb and our breath made white clouds. The air was cold and hurt the lungs. But what air it was! Bright-edged and clean, in the mouth it was like the pure water that bubbled from mountain springs I knew as a boy. Everywhere there was the light, exotic incense of burning piñon. Cedar smoke also drifted through the crisp air, like delicate perfume. The sunshine was as keen as the air, giving every shadow sharp definition like the black-and-white designs on Acoma or Zia pottery.

Except for a pueblo elder who was guarding the entrance to the plaza, none of the Indians spoke, at least not to tourists. Some stood around smoldering bonfires scattered here and there in the plaza, the remains of the previous night's blazing luminaria. Others stood together on the rooftops where the full winter sun provided a little bit of warmth.

What colors that sun shone on! Tourists in brightly colored ski clothes. The intense blue of the sky and the deep green of old pine forests. Most of the rooftop watchers wore brightly striped blankets, brilliant red, yellow, green, orange and blue, all standing together. It all reminded me of Erna Ferguson's photographs; the buildings still looked the same, the people looked the same, the plaza looked the same. Her pictures are black and white, but the colors, too, must have been the same.

Long before the dancers were ready to begin, the Taos clowns began to emerge from doorways and alleyways to mingle with the spectators. A tourist near us laughed and asked one of the clowns who he was, what he represented, but received only a stony stare in reply. These are sacred clowns: they are not to be spoken to, or touched, or bothered in any way during this ceremonial. They act as policemen, in case some visitor has been rash enough to come into the plaza carrying a camera or cell phone or some liquor. Their expressionless silence is a reminder that the ceremony demands sacred respect. At Taos these men are called *Chiffoneta* or *Black Eyes*. Elsewhere they may be referred to as *koshares*. They wear dark pants, or leggings and breechclouts in the old manner, and sometimes they wear a kind of sleeveless poncho made of burlap or rough cloth. Others are naked above the waist.

Chiffoneta paint themselves with wide black and white stripes. One stripe goes across the eyes, like a mask; one crosses the chin; several wrap around the arms and legs; and two or three wrap around the chest and belly. To make "fancy" headdresses for the ceremonial, Chiffoneta take big clumps of cornhusks and straw and wrap them up in their hair. The idea, apparently, is to look as silly as possible, and as wild. But do not be too deceived by these headdresses. When the Chiffoneta dance and the tall golden crowns sway and weave in the bright sun, it is like a field of autumn corn moving in the wind.

From our snow pile vantage point, we could see in both directions, into the plaza and also behind us toward the buildings and the frozen stream. There came a series of loud declamations followed by some kind of commotion. Turning around, we suddenly found ourselves witnesses to a happening I had previously only read about. A Chiffonet initiation was taking place less than a hundred feet away.

It began with a cacique making a long speech from one of the roofs, yelling so that his words would echo off the other apartment (and off Blue Mountain behind it, I would swear). As his declaration neared its climax, three Chiffoneta came out of a doorway, holding a man between them. They led him to one of the open stretches of the ice-bound stream, where he stripped to the waist and washed himself in the freezing water.

The Chiffoneta helped him cleanse himself by piling snow on his back and rubbing it in. Then all four vanished back through the doorway, returning by a secret route to their kiva to continue the initiation. We watched as this happened four times, to four different men. Then three babies were brought out. Each time, a Chiffonet carried the bundled-up infant to the stream, softly singing a chant as he walked. The Chiffonet dipped ice water with his palm and applied it to the baby's head.

Afterward, two Indian boys decided it was time for them to try taunting the clowns. They ran up close to one and made faces at him. They threw snowballs at another. I noticed that the boys were being careful not to speak to the Chiffoneta. The Chiffoneta were also mute as they set out in pursuit of these little demons, and remained absolutely silent while dragging them back to the stream. One little boy submitted to his punish-

The Christmas Deer Dance at Taos Pueblo

ment bravely and wordlessly. He stripped off his parka and sweater and shirt and took his ice-water dousing like a brave warrior. The other boy kept resisting and trying to pull away, but it only made matters worse for him. Two Chiffoneta picked him up and threw him into the stream, clothes and all.

The two little boys hurried past us on their way home for dry clothes, shivering and solemn.

And now we began to notice men coming into the plaza, one here and one there, quietly passing through the spectators. We would not have known they were the dancers, since they were dressed in Levi's and wore heavy parkas like everyone else in New Mexico, except that each one was alone, and each carried a white bundle from which protruded a set of antlers.

Quietly, unobtrusively, they went to their separate kivas to make their preparations. More time passed while we stamped our feet to keep the blood flowing. The drumming would stop awhile, then begin again. The people standing around the plaza and on the roofs talked with one another in hushed voices, making a low humming sort of sound in the winter air. But then a ripple of silence began in the people nearest the north building. It spread toward us. Faces turned in unison toward the quiet. The line of spectators began to part, opening a passageway between colored parkas and striped blankets.

The women of the Deer Dance had come.

So subtle was their appearance on the plaza that they seemed to have simply materialized, already forming into two long lines as they passed by the spectators. The lines flowed into their timeless pattern and became living walls of a passageway, a corridor of women facing each other.

Drummers came next, men with heavy drums who took up their places at the end of the human corridor, sealing it off. The drumsticks rose with sacred deliberation, then fell, and the heartbeat of the Deer Dance had begun again as it has done every midwinter for generations long ago lost to human memory.

It is a slow, steady, mesmerizing rhythm, that drumming of Taos. It is a rhythm that carries with it distant memories of waterfalls somewhere back in lonely cañons of the Sangre de Cristo mountains. It brings to mind the pulsing of the wind at the mouth of a cavern. It echoes the beat of the human heart, the heartbeat as it would be heard from inside the heart itself. Hearing it, you might start to make a comment to someone standing near you and forget what it was you wanted to say. You might forget you have other appointments in other places. The beat seems to put you in touch with your own pulse until it is the only thing you are really aware of.

The two lines of women begin to move. In response to the slow, insistent throb of the drums, they bend their knees slightly, in unison, bending and straightening gracefully in time with the drums. Clowns swagger and stumble into the dance corridor, their movements a caricature of dancing, deliberately contrasting with the soft elegance of the deer women. A clown stands in front of one of the women, his fat belly with its white and black stripes almost touching her. He demonstrates fancy dance steps for her. He leers. He is very clumsy, and very funny. Another clown puts his hands up behind his scarecrow headdress and gyrates in a burlesque hula, grinning at several women at once.

The women do not smile. Their dark eyes remain fixed on the women in the facing line. Their hands remain motionless. They remain in perfect posture, erect, simply bending at the knees to rise and fall slightly to the drums, the insistent, timeless beat of the drums.

The dresses of the women are modest and elegant. They are of a single plain color, usually bright blue, bright red or bright green. A few are brilliant turquoise, orange or purple. They are simple columns of fabric that slightly accentuate the bosom then fall straight to the ankles in one clean line. One shoulder is bare. Down the back of the dress is its only decoration, a narrow ribbon accented by woven designs or silver fetishes.

Their lustrous black hair is very long, kept in place on either side with a silver clip or a velvet ribbon just over the ear. When they move, their hair seems to undulate downward like a waterfall of liquid jet. Their boots are white doeskin, soft as chamois and white as writing paper, wrapped upward from the ankle to midcalf. In each hand, each woman holds a freshly cut fir bough upright in front of her, keeping her elbows held tightly to her side as if fastened there. All the while she continues the dipping movement, body held regally erect, her knees making the only movement, bending in rhythm to the drumbeat filling the plaza.

❧

Two more women now appeared, women whose costumes symbolize their special role in the ceremony. The other women defered to them. Like the others, they wore plain long dresses with one shoulder left bare, except that their dresses were dazzling white. Their hair was loosely wrapped and pinned up, crowned with a fan or corona of long feathers to mark their ceremonial nobility. In one hand, each held an evergreen bough. In the other, a gourd rattle. None of the watching Indians spoke, but they looked at one another knowingly and then back at the two women in white. These are the women chosen to be the Deer Mothers.

They took their place in front of the drum circles and the Chiffoneta appeared again. This time, however, there was a difference. The clowns now carried weapons in the form of very short toy bows, with "arrows" made of long pieces of straw. They made no move against the two who represented sacred deer, but postured like mighty hunters for the benefit of the other women. They showed off their weapons, searched the ground for deer tracks while moving to the beat of the drums, flexed their muscles and sniffed the air. The women took no notice, but went on moving with the drum rhythm.

Suddenly the two hunters appeared. One moment they were not there and the next moment they were moving among the Chiffoneta. Somewhere near me a woman gasped softly, for these were strong, well-built young men. Their costumes were soft white leather kilts and short ponchos. Because they were hunting they wore no face paint or body decorations. Each had a single feather in his hair and carried a longbow and quiver of arrows. They did not dance but stood near the Deer Mothers, wary and watchful.

The dance became mesmerizing, the demanding drums and the slow fluidity of the dancing women. With conscious effort I blinked my eyes as if awakening from a dream, and to regain my sense of where I was I looked up over the heads of the dancers at the surrounding rooftops. The Indians in their brightly colored blankets were still there, lined up everywhere on the different levels, silently looking down at the dancers. As I was gazing upward, still getting myself oriented, I saw every head turn toward the adobe wall that encloses the plaza and connects the two buildings.

The animals were coming.

According to legend, this is the time of year when the spirits of the animals come to dance with the people. It is recognition of the cycle of life that calls for the four-leggeds to die in order that the two-leggeds may live. The deer and elk and buffalo and antelope eat the grass; in their turn, their flesh feeds the people. The Deer Dance is a formal, ritualized, self-conscious acknowledgment, a humble acknowledgment of the natural way of things. It glorifies the animals and the relationship; it pays honor to the sacredness of both. Some of the people act out the role of the animals, who endure; others act out the hunt, which is timeless.

The adobe wall came alive with animals. The bodies were hidden behind it, so all I saw were animal heads in a strange-looking procession along the top of the wall, moving toward an opening into the plaza. The heads dipped and rose to the throb of the big drums. Antlers rattled together. As they drew closer to the opening I felt a chill in my spine that had nothing to do with being cold.

The animals were coming. Deer heads, bobbing, shy, wary, looking about; elk holding their heads high and their antlers back, proud, ready to run or challenge; antelope making stiff and sudden movements, wide-eyed and alert; buffalo heads, ponderously swaying slowly from side to side.

As they entered the plaza I saw that they were men wearing animal heads. Their bodies were covered with animal hides and they walked bent over, using short sticks as forelegs, moving to the drums, each man moving in the manner of the animal he represented. Cautiously but without breaking the rhythm of the drums, they moved toward the corridor of women, the hunters and the Deer Mothers.

Each deer or elk or buffalo danced to the same beat, but each danced in his own way. They passed between the women, weaving in and out of the line as they danced toward the edge of the plaza and back again. Their feet, rising and falling to the hammering drums, moved as if the animals were wild in the forests. Some appeared to be grazing as they danced. Others made quick sideways motions as if running or fighting.

Then, in obedience to some silent signal, the animals came to the people. Giving over their individual patterns and solitary dancing, they became more somber and made their way down the corridor between the lines of women. There they stopped. Still moving slightly to the drums, they stood in two lines facing the women.

Now, poised and regal in their white dresses, the two Deer Mothers began moving along the lines. Their dancing consisted only of bending slightly at the knees, dipping slightly and rising again without expression. As she came to each animal, a Deer Mother raised her gourd rattle high overhead; when it stopped rattling, she brought it down silently. The animal sank to its knees and stayed motionless. Down the line the women went, dancing, obeying the drum, putting the animals down. After reaching the end, the Deer Mothers returned along the lines, but now the rattle was silent and they presented the evergreen boughs. As the bough was lifted before him, the animal rose to his feet.

The symbolism was as hypnotic as the insistent drums. The dry seeds inside the gourds represent autumn, the harvest, the time of gathering food for the people. The rattle is alive with noise and then it falls silent, but the seed within is still viable. Like the seeds, the deer represents life whose time has come and who will be harvested to feed the people. The evergreen is the people's way of acknowledging that the plants do not die from being harvested, nor does the deer. New life returns, always. It is a rhythm. It is a cycle. If it is paid homage to in a sacred manner, it will continue forever.

By silent accord triggered, by some signal too subtle for spectators to see, the Deer Mothers command that the ritual be repeated. And then again. Three times the animals come before the women, and three times they are made to slump to the earth and are raised up again.

It is a serious, sacred ritual, but pueblo dancers are not without a sense of humor. Life is not always deliberate and grim. As the pounding of the drums kept on spreading the mood of solemnity and mystery, the clowns kept on clowning. Against the serious-looking mask worn by the Deer Dancers, the Chiffoneta put on the comic mask to remind people that the truths of life can wear two faces. Sometimes things are funny, sometimes serious.

Chiffoneta love to tease the tourists. One who had a particularly demonic look on his striped face came and stood in front of me. He pointed to the blanket I had draped over my arm. Then he pointed to his chest, which was bare. I ignored him. He persisted. I went on ignoring him, but when it became evident that he was not going away, I gave him the blanket.

And what did he do with it? He flung it down on the snow, at my feet, and sat down crosslegged on it. He pretended he was a tourist, looking everywhere, pointing excitedly at nothing at all, snapping pictures with an imaginary camera, looking impatiently at his imaginary wristwatch, then yawning and eating imaginary popcorn. Eventually he got up and went away to torment someone else, leaving my blanket where it lay. I got the message, or rather the trio of messages. One was that blankets, like fire and bread and meat, are to be shared. The second was that it is better to be the dancer than the passive spectator. The third? It was a reminder that to sit upon the ground, even caked with hard snow, was to put oneself back in touch with the essential, the real.

When it comes to the dance ritual, one primary role of the Chiffoneta is that of despoilers. Brash and rude, they attempt to disrupt the proceedings and carry off the deer and other animals. They would like to be free to shoot all the animals they can and then make away with the meat, paying no regard either to the spirit of the animal or to the ritualized rules of the pueblo. And *that* is where the two real hunters come in. They are there to stand guard over the dancing animals and protect them from selfish and reckless clowns. But these hunters in white kilts and white ponchos are not men, especially not policemen or wardens: they are mountain spirits, each one a kind of katsina responsible for seeing to it that no life is taken without the proper rituals.

Sometimes, the clowns form a pack and rush the hunter-guards. While some keep the mountain spirits busy, a few others get through and into the dance corridor. There they go up to a deer or elk person and "shoot" him with straw arrows. They do it without ritual, without asking the animal's permission, so the crowd on the rooftop is permitted to shout disapproval.

Once the animal has been shot, the clown's labors begin in earnest. His friends help to load the "dead" animal onto his back—even if the man wearing the animal head weighs more than the clown—and the clown must now make his escape from the vigilance of the hunters and the Deer Mothers. He has to carry his kill out of the corridor and outrun the guards, somehow making it back to one of the kivas hidden deep in the alleys of the pueblo.

That chilly Christmas, very few clowns escaped with their kills. With all of the jostling and the heavy costumes and antlers, many ended up with bruises and bumps. The laughter and clowning continued in spite of it all. The hunters remained even-tempered, the women remained impassive (except for a few who giggled when a clown slipped in the snow and fell under the weight of his two hundred–pound load), and those who abused the sacred souls of the animals were roundly chastised.

I do not know how long I stood there in the snow, watching. Time lost meaning. Even toward the close of the ceremonial, late in the afternoon, something spiritual seemed to be keeping the material world at arm's length.

☙

A few days earlier, driving in the car on our way to Taos, we talked about the cold weather and the snow and wondered how it would affect the dance. We talked about the tourists, too, hoping the place would not be clogged with curiosity seekers. I silently told myself that I would be totally, completely happy if I could see but a single special sight at the Christmas Deer Dance, if I could have just a single vivid memory to take home. As it happened, I took home far, far more.

The Christmas Deer Dance at Taos Pueblo

The first memory I took home actually happened the evening before. We had planned to witness the pueblo's Christmas Eve processional and ended up missing the night's main event.

Deep snow choked the narrow road leading into Taos Pueblo, forcing everyone who had come to see the Procession of the Virgin to park a mile away and walk. We arrived too late to see the procession of the statue from the church into the plaza; however, the bonfires in the plaza, the *luminaria,* still burned brightly. Families build the fires to illuminate the Virgin's progress as she is paraded around the village, and by tradition the fires are also signals to wayfaring strangers who are invited to share the warmth and partake of food.

By the time we got there the Virgin was back on her altar inside the church, but the luminaria were still blazing finely. I bought fry bread, fresh and fragrant from the wood-fired ovens, and we accepted a young couple's invitation to share their bonfire.

Other bonfires threw dancing shadows against the adobe buildings. Piñon and cedar crackled as they burned, filling the cold air with an aroma like incense. All up and down the valley and across the fields, the snow made a perfect blanket of white. The sky was deep as ever skies can be, crystal clear and studded with stars. In front of me, under the stars and above the snow, loomed the sacred blue mountain of Taos. I began to say, to our hosts as well as to our friends, what a shame it was that we had missed the Virgin's procession. But my words were cut short, for at that very moment, burning across the frigid azure sky over the sacred mountain, streaked the brightest meteor I have ever seen.

That, I thought, was going to be my Taos memory. I would be content with it.

The next day, however, other things happened. I have said how the drums seemed to pull us into the walled plaza, where we stood on piles of snow waiting for the dance to begin. I had been wishing the bright sunshine would have just a little more warmth in it. I shivered and said to one of my friends, "When do you think this thing will get started?"

As if in remonstrance for my impatience, three black crows flew over the pueblo in formation. They appeared in the sky just as I spoke. And in that same moment, the drums began.

So I had a second memory to take with me. Then came a third one, and again it began before the drums started to beat. I had been observing my fellow Anglo tourists and noticed how some of them seemed bent on outdoing the others. When they spoke, they seemed to adopt poses. They preened and fussed with their clothing, always adjusting their expensive fur coats or fashionable parkas. They talked about ski trips to Europe. I heard one comparing her Mercedes with her husband's Range Rover. Another one kept smoking cigarettes, holding them in that artificial way people do when they are sure they are being "seen."

But gradually something happened. As the cold deepened and the time passed, those ego-riven fellow tourists began to lose their individualism and started to blend into a homogenized mass, right before my eyes. The colors softened and the outlines blurred as if the spectacle were turning into an impressionist painting. I had no sooner noticed it than the effect was complete and I could no longer identify any of them as individuals. Which one smoked cigarettes, and which one had the Mercedes? Soon after that, the drums began again. Then the Deer Mothers appeared and, in their presence, all individual faces seemed to vanish. For those few hours all of the watchers became a timeless, shapeless mass.

Finally, there is the memory of the shadows.

At the end of the second dance the dancers withdrew from the plaza in a processional, moving back toward kivas somewhere in the forbidden recesses of the houses. When they came back along the adobe wall to make their appearance for the third dance, it was late afternoon. The low sun slanted across the plaza, turning adobe into pure gold. Some deer dancers were standing out of sight, but I could see their shadows on the wall of the building. The sun threw two long parallel shadows I recognized as ladderpoles from a kiva. And then the shadow picture became animated with the sharp-edged silhouettes of antlers moving and bobbing. They passed on along that building, coming toward us; now the shadows became the bulky shapes of bison heads, deer heads, elk heads.

I knew what the shadows were: they were men wearing costumes. But the drums and the Deer Mothers had already worked their change in me, for I could also believe that they were *not* men. I knew they were not real animals, yet neither were they ordinary men. What were these shadows, these forms? For one brief moment I knew what it must be like to believe they were the mountain spirits of the deer, the spirits of the four-leggeds, coming up out of the kivas and coming down from the sacred blue mountain at Christmas to dance among the believing people.

The Christmas Deer Dance at Taos Pueblo

INTRODUCTION TO *In Search of Essence*

More Water, Fewer Mountains

> *Though changed, no doubt, from what I was when first*
> *I came among these hills; when, like a roe,*
> *I bounded o'er the mountains, by the sides*
> *Of the deep rivers, and the lonely streams,*
> *Wherever nature led.*
>
> —William Wordsworth, "Tintern Abbey"

Like many mountain kids, I developed an early prejudice against anywhere flat. Every summer the tourists would come with their stories of driving across Kansas or Nebraska in sweltering heat. We overheard complaints about the highways crossing Iowa and Illinois and Texas until it became evident to us that there was just no point in going anywhere you couldn't see mountains.

Then came a female from the flatlands, the Nebraska brunette who decided I would marry her. And on our first trip together to the east coast of Nebraska to meet her family, I realized the peaceful beauty of those rolling hills with their narrow shady creeks, the wonder of rich black earth, the magic of fireflies, and the tang of mulberries. As the years passed I drove the prairie highways many times. Literary interests took me into regions described by Cather, Neihardt, Sandoz and Eiseley. I met Mildred Bennett of Red Cloud and Stan Smith of Minden, friendships that led to camping on a tallgrass prairie and watching birds on the Platte River.

Then came the canoe. A story by Willa Cather made me want to explore the Republican River on the border between Nebraska and Kansas, so I found a friend who owned a canoe and off we went. It wasn't long before I began looking for a canoe of my own. I was hooked, hypnotized, bewitched by the glide of the keel and the ripples vanishing off on either side, by the quiet dip of the paddles and the wooded riverbanks slipping by. I heard stories of magic canoe places that lay far to the north, across many miles of prairie, places with names like the Boundary Waters and the Quetico Wilderness. Inevitably came the day when I had to lash my canoe to the top of my pickup, turn my back to the mountains, and go discover what these Boundary Waters were all about.

In Search of Essence

Wilderness camping can come as a shock to some, but it's a boring kind of shock. Thanks to our modern ultralight equipment, we no longer have to spend time cutting boughs for our beds, hauling firewood, and finding long straight saplings for tent poles. Thanks to modern fabrics, we don't have to sit in camp waxing our boots or drying our wool socks. Everything has become so simple that there's little to do in camp except sit around wondering what to do. Those who are new to it can find it sort of nerve-wracking. One answer to the question of how to approach the wilderness comes from Marcus Aurelius, the Stoic philosopher who was emperor of Rome between AD 161 and 180. He advises us to "look to the *essence* of a thing" (*Meditations VIII 22*). A couple of years ago I followed his suggestion during a canoe trip in the Boundary Waters Canoe Area Wilderness. For those who have been to the BWCAW, we were on a route from the Chainsaw Sisters Saloon to Basswood Lake.

This is my method for staying in touch with essence. Several times during any given day I might lay my paddle across the gunwales and dig into my shirt pocket for my stubby pencil and water-stained notepad, letting the canoe drift slowly along. In its wake, ripples make lazy V's across tree reflections in the still water. Or, trudging on a long portage through the woods, I might come to an open space where there's room to lift and twist the canoe off my shoulders and sit a moment to catch my breath.

Out comes the pencil stub and notepad. I write down a single word or perhaps a phrase or two.

"The sound of walking with your head inside a boat."

"Spruce trees, upside down in reflection."

"Blueberries!"
"One loon, then silence."
"Packing for the trip—choosing stuff—the old familiar feel of things."
"Supper under tarp."
"Smooth lip of waterfalls."

Just a few words, meaningless to anyone who was not there with me, but when I look at them later on, they trigger the day's memories better than a photograph. Without the notebook there would be fewer memories, and without the memories my wilderness trek loses all essence and therefore all meaning. If I forget that lonely cry of a single loon or the sweet firmness of ripe blueberries, the reflections on the water, eating supper under a tarp in the rain, then I will have done nothing during that week except lug an eighteen-foot canoe and a fifty-pound pack from lake to lake for no better reason than to give my butt an occasional ride.

This is how it works. Each evening there will be a camp, some kind of supper to cook, some chance to lean back against a tree or rock or zip myself into the tent, and write in the journal. The term is from a French word, *jour,* meaning "day." What kind of day did I have? I dig out my 9x12 notebook, bent and dog-eared from being carried in the pack. I retrieve the notepad from my shirt pocket and turn my terse phrases and single words into longer sentences and paragraphs. And I have to do it every "jour" or else I find the memory bytes have gone down the dumper along with my recollection of French.

The evening before setting out for Ely, Minnesota, to start my annual canoe trip, this is what I wrote in my notebook:

"Today was the packing, the laying out of paddles, tent and sleeping bag, ropes and stuff sacks. There was the replenishing of the toiletry kit, checking the water pump, tarp, and stove. Ah, the stove! Touching the metal and smelling the lingering odor of white gas fuel brings back the familiar sense of anticipation, the languid impatience to be gone, on the road, back on the lakes again. . . . Touching these familiar things makes them seem romantic, special.

"And so the essence *of today, the first day of this year's canoe adventure,"* the journal continues, *"is the romance I find contained in metal and wood, in ripstop nylon and heavy canvas."* Romance isn't always about sending flowers and steaming up car windows. It's about daydreams. It's about anticipation.

In other years and on other trips, I've made notes about different species of trees I encountered, the difficulties of the portages, the scenery

In Search of Essence

along the way, and the wildlife. But when I revisit those journals and notebooks I find them about as interesting as old grocery lists. Sixteen species of trees. Slept on three kinds of rock, none of which I can identify. No ripe berries. No campfires because of rain. These notes offer me nothing to remember except facts, and facts, like technology, can deaden human imagination.

Those notebooks full of facts remind me of the summers I spent behind the wheel of a refitted U.S. Army 6x6, hauling tourists into Rocky Mountain "backcountry." Cameras with motor drives had just come on the market. At various places along the logging roads, I would click on my microphone and announce something like "On your right, just ahead, there is a large growth of *Arctostaphlyus uva-ursi*—common kinnikinnick. . . ." And even before I had finished my sentence, cameras would begin snapping and whirring like a swarm of deranged locusts. When the tourists got their pictures back from the drugstore weeks later, they probably asked themselves why they had seventeen shots of a bunch of small green leaves.

Forget the camera. If you have a journal entry saying "Christmas tree expedition in December, a whole grocery sack full of bright green kinnikinnick with crimson berries, hot chocolate on the truck's tailgate, kids sledding, laughter and frosty breath," then you have a memory. And no photo is necessary.

This year in the Boundary Waters Wilderness, I gave my notebooking and journaling a different spin. Instead of writing down all the names of the lakes and rivers, and the types of plants and rocks and animals, as if I were planning to make it into a Power Point presentation for Rotarians, I tried to find each day's unique essence, the one quality that gave it special meaning among all the other days spent on the lakes. I did it for an audience that would not need pictures and sound bites.

Myself.

The essence of the days spent in preparation for the trip was romantic nostalgia brought on by handling equipment again, remembering past summers and looking forward to the next new set of lakes and rivers. I filled the little Svea stove, remembering the sound of it sputtering and roaring under a pot of coffee. I packed the coffee knowing how it would smell and taste in an early morning, beside a lake in the wilderness, with fog slowly rising off the water.

The second day involved driving for ten or eleven hours along the interstate. There was no essence to be found in miles-per-gallon or in the number of restroom stops per quart of coffee. But I did find myself changing a little with each mile that took me closer to the BWCAW. A kind of metamorphosis began the instant I pointed the truck toward the wilderness.

Metamorphosis. Possibly the most wonderful mystery in nature.

Lost somewhere in the dozens of file drawers full of potential landfill material that I call my files there is an essay about the metamorphosis of butterflies. The writer describes how these "two-animal animals" change from worm to winged creature. He pictures the process as a series of internal earthquakes in which the organs crumble like dry crackers as every cell of the worm undergoes massive transformation, straining and pushing against the cocoon. Suddenly the fabric of its confinement rips apart and it finds itself with wings, clinging to the remnants of its shell while some old instinct whispers, "Crawl along the branch to safety" and another, newer impulse says, "Let go of the branch and fly!"

Driving wilderness-ward, I watched how roadside scenery went through its gradual transitions. I crossed eastern Colorado's flat brown acres where the principal crops seem to be dust and Republicans; next, I entered eastern Nebraska's loamy black fields and rolling wooded hills. A brief stop in Omaha to sleep and pick up the rest of the crew, and by morning we were speeding through Iowa's picture-worthy farmland. We turned north toward Minnesota and began to see forests of birch and conifer. Mile by mile I was emerging from my urban cocoon, going through a kind of metamorphosis. I no longer needed to listen to the radio, but was content to listen to the tires on the road instead. I no longer cared if the truck was dirty and cluttered. In the city, I wash my truck once a week, and each day I unload whatever I happen to be carrying in it. If ever there is a cult for Virgo neatness freaks, I could qualify as High Priest. But heading for the wilderness waters I somehow become indifferent to rain-specked dust, mud and insect splats on the paint job. I take arrogant pride in pulling into a rest stop driving my pickup with its jumble of camping gear, and a long-hulled canoe strapped on the roof.

~

We arrived at North Country Canoe Outfitters, just outside Ely, late in the evening. Our hostess, Kathy Schiefelbein, wanted to know what time we would be up for breakfast. Seven-thirty, I said, and awoke next morning to find my watch just turning seven-twenty-five. "Behind schedule already!" I said. "Need to hurry up!" But breakfast was unhurried, a matter of coffee kept warm on a hotplate and rolls and cereal ready anytime.

I was still thinking in terms of schedule, clock time, "tasking." After breakfast, I quizzed John Schiefelbein in detail, poring over three maps, trying to mark all the portage details, making sure I knew about all the rapids, asking him about fishing gear and equipment. I asked him three times how to get to the launch site.

But at day's end, guess what? All was simple. I turned off the highway where John said I should, drove to the next road, took it to a logging road, followed the logging road ten or twelve miles, and ended up in the parking lot of the Chainsaw Sisters Saloon. Within a half hour we had the eighteen-foot Jensen canoe in the water and loaded to go, ready for the paddle down to Mudro Lake.

Back home, the packs had seemed huge, heavy, and complicated with inventory—is the stove in this one or that? where's the toilet paper? should a rain jacket be on top?—but at the launch they simplified themselves into just four waterproof packs sitting so compactly in the canoe they scarcely showed above the gunwales. The bow-to-stern balance was perfect.

Before we launched, I had to take out my notepad and pencil to write just one word under "Launch Day": *simplify.*

"Simplify," said Henry David Thoreau, a fellow boater. Henry liked to drift around Walden Pond in a leaky rowboat, peering over the side in hopes of discovering the underwater behavior of loons. That was Henry's way of working for a living. One boat, one lake, one loon were enough for him. "I had three chairs in my house," he wrote, "one for solitude, two for friendship, three for society."

I had three pairs of socks—one for the canoe, another for portages, another to wear around camp—but found that I only used two of them. In camp, we had one tent and one small tarp to sit under. One bowl apiece, along with one spoon and one cup. It says here in one of my daily journal entries—if you'll overlook the redundancy of "daily journal"—that I needed to simplify the number of worries I brought along to the BWCAW. I had started out with quite a few, but while crossing Nebraska I began sorting them out and repacking them.

With a few strokes of the paddles, the truck and the Chainsaw Sisters Saloon disappeared behind us. I was down to just two worries to lug along on the trip, and one of them was that I was starting to forget what it was I needed to be worrying about. The other was more practical: course and distance. Where we were going and how long it would take.

On the evening of that first day's paddling, an evening drizzle turned into a steady night of rain. We ate supper under the tarp, sitting on uneven ground and trying not to brush the fabric with our heads, which would cause moisture to leak through. We ate an uncomplicated hot supper of macaroni and cheese with dried tomato, dried chicken and chorizo cubes. Dessert consisted simply of dried apples and berries, rehydrated in a tin cup. And it was as good as it was simple.

As dark came on, we zipped ourselves into the tent and sat cross-legged on sleeping mats playing gin rummy. On paper I lost over $300, but it was a problem easily solved: tomorrow I'd simply charge my tentmate $300 fare for riding in my canoe. The rain kept up, the floor seams leaked, and puddles formed under the sleeping pads. But to look on the bright side of things, I wouldn't have to go down to the lake to fill the water pot in the morning.

Morning brought more rain, so we cooked under the tarp and stayed there most of the day. We were not without entertainment, though. We had our coffee and watched a pair of loons with their baby swimming around in the rainy lake. My notes say, cryptically, that the essence of this day was "compression." All the loons in the world and all the wild things of the BWCAW seemed compressed into just that one family of loons. It was all we needed. All our human need of comfort was compressed into a few square feet of dry space beneath a green tarp and a steel mug of coffee held between the hands.

I bought a couple of "compression" bags for this trip, the first time I'd ever used them. The sleeping bag goes in one, clothes in another, and when I cinch down the nylon straps, a sack the size of a bed pillow suddenly becomes a hard little package the size of a football. The weight stays the same, but the stuff takes up less room and is easier to organize.

At Fourtown Lake that rainy day, according to the journal, I found everything can be compressed. The view from under the tarp showed me one gull, one family of loons, and one lake with rain falling. There was one little island out there—canoe people know the kind—rimmed with gray rock, accented with lichen and moss, softened with willow and birch, dark with conifers, resting on its own blurred reflection in the lake. I dubbed it Everyisland.

Over here—you need to pretend I'm pointing with my coffee mug and have my pencil stub sticking out between my first two fingers—over here is the United States Forest Service fire grate of heavy iron and two logs for seats, the same simple setup that you find in most of the BWCAW campsites. Over there—I'm pointing again—is a flat-branched cedar and a birch with axe and knife scars on it. It's every campsite I've ever been in, will ever be in, and in my imagination I can arrange it and then rearrange it. I can mentally move it to Seagull Lake or Knife Lake, put it on the Kawawishi River or Burntside or Crab Lake. By compressing it into a beat-up 9x12 notebook, I can even carry it home with me.

A few days later I was carrying the Jensen canoe and packs over that long portage to Upper Basswood Falls. It was a hot day with punishing sunshine and just enough bugs to be distracting. The portage I had quizzed John about so assiduously turned out to be a simple matter of sore shoulders, stubbed toes, and a sweat-soaked hatband. I walked and carried and walked and carried until my sixty-plus old muscles said, "Enough, already!" and then I rested.

Simple.

"Portage blueberries" says the notepad. The deep shadowy gloom of the forest suddenly opened up into a sunny clearing in the trees, so I raised the bow of the canoe and craned my stiff neck to have a look around. Up until then, the only thing I was looking at was my own boots stumbling over the rocks. The clearing gave me a chance to flip the canoe off into the bushes and take a break. With my back still bent from the long haul, I flopped down on a log.

Blueberries! Blueberries everywhere, darkly ripe and large and sweet by the handful. The next person up the trail found me down on hands and knees, foraging like a cinnamon bear dressed in canoe pants and wearing a baseball cap, stuffing berries into my mouth.

"Get away!" I growled at her. "These are mine. All of them. Go find your own."

"I've got the stoves and food in *my* pack," she reminded me.

"Alright," I mumbled through my mouthful of berries. "You can have those berries way over there. But these are mine."

At that portage's end, we had an eagle sighting, and birdsongs, and water blue as the sky leading ever further into wilderness. At evening, the dropping sunlight became hard and brilliant on the shoreline across the lake as an orange moon rose in the pale sky, a promise of a moonlit night to come. *"Blueberry portage,"* says the journal. *"Eagle and orange moon."*

"The Jensen canoe lies in a bed of grass along the shore and fish are rising in the glassy bay," the journal reads the next day. It's a prosaic description, but at least it was no trouble to write. Just details. No metaphors, no

symbolism. I even used several standard clichés that day, just to save myself the trouble of finding fancy adjectives: *smug satisfaction, reward for effort, pain and gain,* that sort of thing. But finally, I think the day's essence was just my readiness, my willingness, to *accept* these basic rewards as return for my effort.

The next day's essence was the essence of *green*. Had I brought along a kid or two, I would have made them sharpen their outdoor eyes by telling them to observe (and write down) as many shades of green as they could find. And textures of green, too—glossy green, powdery green, sticky green, wet green, old green. You who have paddled the Boundary Waters already know them, the leaves, moss, lichen, grass, flower stems; the subtle shades of birch, aspen, fir, spruce, pine, cedar. Write them down, all of them. Later on there might be a quiz.

"More portaging, meeting fellow followers of the way of the paddle," reads the journal. More paddles moving across the solitude and the peacefulness. But the presence of others did not diminish the day. We paddled on and on, sometimes on placid water with a smooth wake flowing out and away behind the Jensen, sometimes facing headwind with the bow rising and falling in choppy waves. We rested in the lee of an island where I had time to open the notepad and write the word "rhythm." That evening I wrote in the journal that it was not just the rhythm of two paddles dipping and pulling together. It was a familiar rhythm of breakfast, cleanup and packing, loading the canoe, launching, landing and portaging. After just a few days on the water it had become easy and natural.

The most metaphysical entry in my journal has to be the one inspired by the sight of Lower Basswood Falls. After the long portages and long paddles, we were, as Meriwether Lewis wrote in his own journal, "saluted with the agreeable sound of a fall of water." He had come to the Great Falls of the Missouri River, that thirteenth day of June in 1805. Two hundred years later, Basswood Falls still has to be reached by canoe and foot.

As I stood on glacier-polished rocks listening to the agreeable sound, the pounding and roaring of the Basswood cataracts suddenly seemed to represent all the other waterfalls to which the old Jensen had taken us. And what I wrote in my notepad was "Why?" Not why does Basswood seem so familiar, so iconic, but why the hell were we *here?*

Just before taking the plunge over the lip of Basswood Falls, the whole lake seems to gather itself into one final display of mirrored fluidity. It reflects an enormous sky. It is perfectly placid. And then, like a roller coaster going over the first big hill, it drops. It pauses for a fraction of a second at the very edge, then rushes over the edge into instantaneous metamorphosis. One moment the water is so serene, so placid, it almost seems like oil. In the next second it rages into flashing, dazzling foam and molten white energy, a power you cannot imagine ever, ever yielding to the engineering pretensions of the human animal.

"Why?" Do we actually trek and portage and paddle all these many miles—rewarded periodically in nothing more than blueberries and eagle cries and the laughter of loons—simply to see such sights as Basswood Falls? Or are there deeper, far more subconscious reasons for our pilgrimages to lakes and streams and waterfalls? Thoreau asked much the same question. His answer was "Contact." We do it to make contact with our earth. "Life consists with wildness," he wrote. "The most alive is the wildest. Not yet subdued to man, its presence refreshes him."

Our human bodies are water, mostly. Water permeates our blood and our flesh. Perhaps it is this water within us that pulls us, even against our will, to wild places where we move barefoot or in sandals down the ancient rocks to stand at the very edge of the moving stream. Toes nearly in the current, eyes wide and all our nerves alert, we could just as well be cave people in animal skins who stand there in mute wonder at the cataract's rumbling chorus. Is there a voice in the roar of the falling waters? Are we awaiting a message from some primeval god whose face we only dimly recall?

~

After a few days of living on Basswood Lake, we made a decision to leave a day early. Rather than push our endurance into another possible day of rain, we would go out. And the essence of that day was *quiet.* We spoke less that morning, said nothing at all about going out. I packed the tent and my gear quietly, pausing sometimes to listen to a bird singing or the water lapping at the rocks. The silence was awkward.

My mind was trying to slow down, even more than it had already done. It made a conscious effort not to let go, not to break the contact. The trip back toward Mudro Lake and the Chainsaw Sisters Saloon was done mostly in silence. Little jokes that seemed funny the day before now seemed to disturb something. There was talk, of course, mostly about which inlet or stream was the one we wanted to take, but it was devoid of excitement.

Crossing Sandpit Lake, we came to a jaw-clenching steep gully of rocks that some mapmaker with a warped sense of humor had labeled "portage." It had the pitched angle of a barn roof. All along the way there were red and green and blue streaks on the sharp rocks where other canoers had dropped or dragged their boats. *"At least it isn't raining,"* says the notepad.

When we finished the portage and finally had our equipment lashed into the Jensen once again, we float out onto Mudro, our last lake. I looked at the map and jokingly remarked that we didn't *need* to return to the Chainsaw Sisters Saloon and our truck. No, I said, we could just make a right-hand turn, take the portage to Fourtown Lake, and do it all over again.

There were chuckles. "I don't think so." "Maybe not today." "I would, but I hear a cold beer calling to me." But in all the talk of being done with the trip, and in all the light chatter of what lay just minutes away—cold beers, soft truck seats, motorized movement toward real showers and different food—in all such banter I could still sense the private quiet of souls who have seen the wilderness from a canoe and who are unwilling to let go of it.

"Seen the wilderness" is an oversimplification, because we did so much more than just see wilderness. We dreamed river dreams. We left slim wakes on blue-silver lakes. We emerged from sleep among forest shadows, blinking in the clean sunlight, and, drawn by voices of unseen gods, we went to stand silent at the edge of the water.

INTRODUCTION TO *The Terminal Imagination*

Travels in the Mind

> As I was walking up the stair
> I met a man who wasn't there.
> He wasn't there again today.
> I wish, I wish he'd stay away.
> —Hughes Means, c. 1939

The next essay is about imagination, that uniquely human attribute that is paradoxically our greatest asset and our worst enemy. Not only can we invent little men who aren't really there, we can imagine wishing we couldn't imagine them in the first place.

Some will assume that this essay is about fear of flying, but it's not. Others might see it as a kind of travelogue—or maybe I should say "travelblog" in the modern parlance of the linguistically handicapped. But it's really about "the little man who wasn't there" phenomenon, about the fascination of watching my own brain shut itself down so it could duck the cerebral paralysis of too much imagining.

I'm not afraid to fly, since I know that my imagination is merely fantasizing about engine seizures, cardiac arrest among the flight crew, and bolts jiggling loose from the wings. I think of possible disasters while simultaneously recognizing the fact that the only place they will happen is inside my own head. The day I quit flying will be the day when I can't imagine things *not* happening.

The Terminal Imagination

Cowardice, as distinguished from panic, is almost always simply a lack of ability to suspend the functioning of imagination.

—Ernest Hemingway, *Men at War*

If anyone should know what cowardice is, it would be Ernest Hemingway. A man who spends his life among combat soldiers, guerilla fighters, big-game hunters and matadors learns something about cowardice and panic. Just one artillery shell in your foxhole or a few moments being chased by a wounded rhino provides just about all the experience you'd ever need to understand the subject.

Cowardice, to paraphrase Hemingway, comes from letting yourself imagine what could happen. Hamlet would agree: the Danish prince calls himself "pigeon-livered." "Resolution is sicklied o'er with the pale cast of thought," says Hamlet, and "conscience doth make cowards of us all." What *is* conscience, after all, except a tendency to consider consequences? One day I stopped to talk to a friend of mine. We were standing in his front yard when a big stray dog happened by. Bob's little terrier, small enough to carry in your coat pocket, came yapping off the porch in a full frontal attack. It looked like a timber wolf being confronted by a hamster with bad hair.

"I guess he don't know he's little," Bob said.

As I resumed my walk, I gave that notion some thought. I mean, here was a tiny terrier ready to attack a beast that could crush him in its jaws. And here I was, much larger and stronger and smarter than the stray dog, but perfectly willing to let it go on about its business. Not only could I imagine being bitten, I could imagine the possible consequences of a dog bite, including bleeding, torn clothing and rabies shots. Now, as observations go this one is about as fascinating as wondering why chimpanzees don't tango. Questions of imagination and fear become more interesting, however, when we add evolution to the equation.

According to most evolution theorists, imagination is the single most important trait setting us apart from most other animals (and nearly all of the vegetables). Somewhere far back in time, our ancestors learned to see connections between things. For instance, most animals would look at a rock and a stick and see them as just that: a rock and a stick. To *Homo sapiens,* however, a rock and a stick added up to a spear. And that same imagination that led them to invent weapons and tools also created just enough cowardice to ensure survival. Imagining what could happen "next" would make a man hesitate before rushing out with his pointy stick to jab a saber-toothed tiger.

Here's another fascinating observation for you: imagination takes place in the brain. And here's one to go with it. In *The Immense Journey,* paleontologist Loren Eiseley points out one way in which the human brain is unique: unlike those of other animals, our brains *triple* in size during our first year of life. While it's not unusual to see a tomato or a zucchini grow to three times its original size in just a few days, in the case of a brain it's almost weird. It's also odd to see how helpless we are while our brain is thus burgeoning. A newborn antelope can run full speed just a few days after being born, but a human infant spends at least a year doing nothing but lying around sucking up milk, its little fat legs pretty much useless for fight or flight. A robin is hatched, and in no time at all it can take to the air and fly. But it takes years before a human's arms become strong enough to lift its own weight.

While the fledgling human is going through years of relative helplessness due to the slow growth of its bones and muscles, its brain is becoming bigger and more complex by leaps and bounds. *Lots* bigger. So big, in fact, that most of the growth of the brain and skull has to take place outside the womb, outside the mother's body. "If it took place in the embryo," writes Eiseley, "man would long since have disappeared from the planet—it would have been literally impossible for him to have been born. As it is, the head of the infant is one of the factors making human birth comparatively difficult."

Now, here are the two troubling evolutionary questions. What do we *need* with a brain so large that it endangers the survival of our species? And what do we actually *do* with it?

The Terminal Imagination

An animal brain—any animal brain—coordinates a small number of fairly simple functions such as eating, sleeping, keeping warm and reproducing. A gerbil's brain performs these functions efficiently, and without growing much larger than a human zit. Our brains, by comparison, seem ridiculously huge when you consider the relatively little work they do. Most of our brain potential goes untapped, like a car battery connected to only the dome light. Is all that excess brain tissue nothing more than an opportunity for pharmaceutical companies to sell headache remedies? Or are we supposed to be *doing* something with it, something connected to the adaptation and survival of the species? That was Charles Darwin's idea. If we've got it, it must be because we need it.

COGITO ERGO GROUNDED

Cogito ergo sum, wrote Descartes. "I think, therefore I am."

I'm not going so far as to admit to a fear of flying, but I will say that I still have reservations about it. Years ago when I fought forest fires, I was with a bunch of smoke-chasers who had an opportunity to fly back to base camp in a helicopter. It was either take the chopper or make a five-mile hike. One of the older guys, Eddy, walked around the machine several times. He studied the little propeller facing sideways at the end of the tail. He looked up at the rotors, which are actually skinny wings that spin round and round.

"Ready to go?" I asked.

"I'm gonna hike," Eddy said. "Any fool can see that this thing can't fly."

Eddy's problem, obviously, was that he had given the matter too much thought. But I didn't think much about it, or any of the many commercial flights I was on, until some years later when my wife and I decided to fly up to Kodiak, Alaska. Maybe my doubts were triggered by Loren Eiseley's book, which I was reading at the time. In any case, the experience of getting to the airport, waiting for the plane, and then making the flight turned into an opportunity to ponder the ways and workings of the human brain. Starting with my own. How, for instance, does my personal capacity for needless worrying fit into the whole evolutionary scheme of things?

All through the night prior to the trip, I lay in the dark imagining the plethora of potential disasters and delays. We might oversleep. Once on the road, we might run into heavy traffic, have a flat, throw a timing belt, burn up the transmission, encounter construction delays, get lost, or even end up at the toll booth without the correct change. There might be fog, ice, forgotten suitcases and forgotten tickets! I won't even begin to list the delays I imagined could happen after we *arrived* at the airport; suffice it to say that they involved terrorists in the parking garage, sadists at the security checkpoint, and people in saffron robes selling flowers.

Giving up on the idea of sleeping, of course, I woke my wife at three in the morning, and in thirty minutes we were on the road. No highway construction projects barred our way. No mechanical failure left us stranded. There was no problem at the toll booth. We arrived at the airport two hours too early, strolled through ticketing and security, and found empty seats—lots and lots of empty seats—in the waiting area. As dawn gradually brought gray light to the eastern horizon, we sat in chilly silence. I had no one to talk to except myself.

In lieu of conversation, I took *The Immense Journey* from my carry-on bag and was reading it when along came two more Alaska-bound passengers. I had just finished Chapter Nine, "Man of the Future," in which Eiseley explains that the size of animal skulls, including those of humans, bears little relationship to intellectual capacity. A bigger skull doesn't necessarily mean more intellect, a fact my wife already suspected.

These two who had entered the waiting area looked as if they might be living examples of what Eiseley was talking about. It was obvious they were sportsmen headed for the wilds of Alaska where the moose and salmon live. Masters of rod and gun, they no doubt were keen trackers and canny woodsmen. Besides plaid flannel shirts and L.L. Bean jackets, both had brand-new matching baseball caps that they had purchased in the airport. Now, as humans go, these two specimens ranked pretty high on the cranial volume scale. One of the hominids put on his cap, declared it too tight, and loosened the adjustable plastic band. He looked to his companion for his opinion.

"Looks tight. How does it feel?"

"Tight."

"Maybe oughta loosen it."

"Yeah."

This adjustment having been accomplished, it was the other one's turn to go through the same procedure, right down to the "yeah."

And it is at this point that you are asking yourself, what does the circumference of hatbands on baseball caps have to do with evolution? It goes back to that thing about the brain, about how it has to triple in size *after* birth because if it grew to almost mature size inside the womb, it would keep the birth from happening.

In baseball hats, I wear a "large," which means my skull is approximately twenty-four inches in circumference. In women that's a nice waist measurement, but you're not going to find the cervix anywhere near that large. Ergo, giving birth to a baby whose brain and skull were fully developed would be like trying to shove a cantaloupe through the hole in a doughnut. It won't work. End of species.

My two specimens of *Homo* sports had large skulls. The adjustable plastic straps had been adjusted out to the very limit and were still causing indentations around the perimeter. The next thing to presume is that all of that space inside the skull is taken up with lots and lots of brain tissue. And that leads back to my first question, which is whether all that brain tissue is actually doing anything besides telling the body when to sleep and feed and how to get warm and procreate.

Consider the evidence. First, my specimens could have bought their caps almost anywhere else, other than in the airport, and would have paid much less for them. Second, these particular caps carried the advertising logo of a well-known Colorado brewery, so we may assume that these two had deliberately paid premium prices in order to become walking billboards for beer. The only reason I could think of for *doing* that was to prove—at any cost—their impeccable taste in malt beverages.

However, as peripatetic beer ads they had yet another problem. Their combined girth, roughly that of a pair of side-by-side refrigerators, showed pretty clearly how a steady diet of beer can cause an overhang sufficient to totally hide the belt buckle, not just from the wearer, but from anyone. The irony—or incongruity—of seeing these two big beer bellies beneath two ads for beer was softened by the fact that they both wore their hats turned around backward. If you were where you could read the beer ad, you couldn't see the beer gut.

If there is some vast and unknown purpose to evolution, did some creative force spend 500,000 years enlarging human brain capacity so that we would wear our hats backward with beer ads on them? What does this have to do with survival and adaptation, outside of maybe fooling a predator into thinking our front side is our back side? "The brim of the hat is looking at me," snarled the hungry saber-toothed tiger. "The brim is meant to shade the eyes, so there must be eyes in the back of that creature's skull. I'd better not try a sneak attack."

The Terminal Imagination

Speaking of saber-toothed cats, why is it that *we* were given a big brain while other animals got to develop long claws, sharp teeth, fast legs, and pungent spray systems? We can't fly, climb trees, dig holes, or even run very fast, so what are we doing surviving? Was it natural selection? Picture, if you will, the courtship of a Stone Age human female. There she stands, resplendent in her animal skins, while two human males fight it out for her hand in whatever passed for marriage back in those days. Will she choose to breed with the strongest one? The quickest one? The one with the best claws? The one with the most hair? No. She obviously chose the one who was wearing his hat backward.

THE PRIMATE IN CONCOURSE B

Morning light finally painted the east in streaks of rose and orange. I sipped at my cardboard cup of delicatessen coffee and found the delicate flavor a little more like bland. We sat in chairs made of fiberglass, those formfitting kind of seats that seem specifically designed to make your butt sweat. My wife had taken over the responsibility of watching for the arrival of our DC10, mostly so that she wouldn't have to listen to me worrying that we'd somehow still miss it.

I was left with nothing to do except think about the perspiration rivulets running down my shorts and the coffee that was audibly eroding my stomach lining. I read some more of Eiseley's book and thought again about his question. What do we *do,* in Darwinian terms, with this brain we've developed?

The waiting area had filled up with people by then, so here we sat, almost two hundred of us, primates to a man—or woman—who have achieved world superiority by virtue of our splendid creative imaginations. And yet, we had all managed, just for this occasion, to put our powerful imaginations on the shelf. We were now unimaginative, complacent victims of a curious form of mental Novocain necessary for "air travel." In order to arrive at Anchorage and then Kodiak, we would willingly submit our big fat brilliant brains to a kind of systematic dumbing-down, a deliberate disorientation.

My own disorientation started two hours before we even got to the airport. It began when we left the familiar streets of our town and started down the interstate highway. The interstate never seems familiar to me no matter how often I drive it. Part of it is caused by the strangeness of the sounds out there. I once owned an elderly pickup with unpredictable engine seizures. Periodically, it would become comatose and leave me walking down the side of the interstate toward the nearest telephone. The decibel level out there was all but unbearable. And not engine noise, either; it was the noise of tires on concrete, a horrible roaring like a cyclone that is always coming on but never arrives.

Inside our new car, however, a recent-model Carsophagus with thick glass and thicker insulation, I couldn't hear traffic noise at all. As my wife wasn't speaking to me, I didn't hear anything. There we were, doing more than seventy miles an hour, and there was almost no noise, no bumping, no wind, no sense of thrust, nothing. It felt as though I could put my feet up on the dashboard and catch a few more winks of sleep while the car took us to the airport. The reality, though—well, to experience what it really sounds like and feels like to move at that speed, put on your roller blades and have somebody tow you down the road at seventy-five per.

The interstate had my senses pretty well anesthetized by the time we got to the airport. Choosing the outlying parking area, I drove up and down a dozen aisles full of identical vehicles to find a niche in which to put our own identical vehicle. The cars looked so much alike that the shuttle bus driver wrote down our location on a ticket. Without those alphabetical coordinates we'd never see location A-B6C or our four-door again.

Now it was the shuttle bus's turn to enhance our disorientation. The windows were darkly tinted; the air was conditioned and smelled like a blend of diesel and pine oil disinfectant; outdoor sounds were muffled. We passengers sat like plastic mannequins, giving each other quick plastic smiles. "Let's not get acquainted," expressions seemed to say. In the darkened and odd-smelling cocoon of a shuttle bus we circled the parking lot again and again in search of other mannequins. By the time the bus headed for the terminal, we were disoriented to the point that not one of us could say with certainty if we were headed west or east or north. Nor did we care, because we assumed we were being taken to the terminal.

Disorientation. Like most terminals, this one is not square. It has curves and angles and passageways that don't look like any other building anywhere on earth. The halls and rooms are not called by their usual names, but are "concourses" and "skyways" and "walkways" instead. Inside this alien surrounding with its unfamiliar terms, oddly enough, you find a heavy overdose of uniformity.

Faceless people in matching uniforms search you and your luggage for suspicious bits of metal you might be carrying, thus removing any chance at all you could prove a danger to yourself. The uniform behind the x-ray scanner looks into the flickering screen and discovers that your carry-on bag contains a roll of antacid tablets, half a pack of chewing gum, five keys on a Mickey Mouse key chain, four tampons or three condoms, two loose buttons, a dead ballpoint pen and a cheap paperback novel. But as soon as you have taken three steps past this checkpoint, you cannot describe the person by whom you had just been so thoroughly searched. Actually, you probably very consciously did not look at that person at all.

There is a weary sameness to all the walls in the terminal. The floors have a sameness. Even with clever designs in the tile and modern patterns there is a weary sameness. The temperature is neutral, the humidity is controlled, and so are the smells and the sounds. Everyone walks through the concourses doing the No-Eye-Contact Zombie Shuffle. When I emerged from a restroom in which men stood studiously not noticing each other, I couldn't remember which way I had been walking or which side of the concourse I was on.

Waiting for the loading process to start, I gradually realized that none of these people were really doing anything, that none of them seemed real. Were these creatures actually computer programmers, salesmen, teachers, and grandmothers from respectable neighborhoods? They seemed like architectural enhancements, lifelike sculptures created by some artist to accessorize the concourse frescoes.

I watched through heavily tinted windows as little tractors noiselessly pulled trains of battered luggage carts in aimless patterns around and under the airplanes. Soundless airplanes came gliding down from the aureate sun like toys dropped by some vernal cherub. Others floated magically up and away from the ground and diminished into flecks of horizon dust. It was a mute pantomime, a bronze-tinted viewing screen without sound.

My plastic fanny sauna reminded me of other such seats in other airports. All the same, those airports. The same "stores" that aren't really like stores, selling the same rolls of candy and the same magazines—not to mention the same souvenir baseball caps—at identical cash registers operated by the almost identical cashiers. The same restrooms have the same number of stalls, and the hand dryers are set to the same interval (which is fifteen seconds too short and you finish drying your hands on your pants). Same tinted windows. Same little tractors and toy airplanes.

The Terminal Imagination

Why, I thought, do we go anywhere? What part of a human's existence is fulfilled or enriched by sitting in a car or a bus or a plane to be taken to a place so much like the one that was left behind?

Our flight finally arrived. Ground crews swarmed out to groom and fuel the DC10. Umbilical hoses were attached, and there was a faint sound of machinery to be heard as one of the uniforms went to the nondescript wall of the waiting area and opened a nondescript door. An artificial voice coming from the acoustical ceiling announced that certain "rows" were now "able" to "load." As our row was announced we got up and walked to the door even though the door did not seem to have a connection with the airplane. Beyond the door was an empty, dark, rectangular hallway. But we sure did want to "load," so we followed the herd of mannequins through the opening.

Did you ever use your imagination to see this moment in cross section? We have just stepped through the outside wall of the building and are two stories above the concrete, walking along a rectangular tube of thin metal. We come to the door in the side of the airplane and step through, not assimilating the fact that it, too, is almost thirty feet off the ground. We next shuffle along single-file in mutual patience, avoiding eye contact with those already seated, until we come to our own pair of narrow seats. The seats are equipped with heavy restraining straps.

I know the purpose and the meaning behind that hypnotic highway journey, that disorienting shuttle bus tour of the outlying parking area, the alien concourses and innocuous doorways leading into loading chutes. Without these devices to numb my mind, I would not get on the airplane. My imagination needs to be shut down. All of our imaginations need to be anesthetized before air transportation of human beings is possible. If we really thought about what we were doing, we wouldn't do it.

Which brings us to the subject of the airplanes themselves.

When I was a boy, it was still possible to drive to the Denver airport, park for free, walk around the outside of the terminal building, and stand at the fence watching the planes come and go. It was also possible to tell them apart. Any kid of my acquaintance could tell a DC3 from a Constellation or a DC4 and could identify a Stratoliner a mile away in thin fog. Today, the planes all look alike or, if they don't, who cares? Most of us don't want to think about it or else we'd start wondering whether the engines mounted on the tail are more apt or less apt to fall off than the ones mounted under the wings.

The Terminal Imagination

Let's go back to our exercise in cross sectioning. If we slice our DC10 right down the center and examine it, we may decide we don't want to visit Aunt Caroline in Spokane after all.

As you know already, once inside and seated you will be strapped into a narrow chair bolted to a metal frame. The metal frame adds rigidity to a pressurized metal tube quaintly referred to as the "cabin" as if it were part of a luxurious cruise ship. Cruise ships, however, are made of very solid steel. The fuselage of the airplane is made of thin metal. In fact, the ratio between this cylinder's volume and the gauge of its material is roughly the same as that of a recyclable aluminum can. These "walls" are upholstered and decorated so you won't start thinking about their actual thickness, but a reasonably strong person could shove an icepick through it.

Our cross-section look at the airplane reveals a long storage compartment beneath the lightweight floor. It is filled to capacity with thousands of pounds of freight, luggage and mail. Remember how you overstuffed your suitcase and how heavy it was? Well, your fellow passengers have all done the same thing. Some of them brought along so much weight they needed to rent baggage carts in order to get it to the check-in counter. Others resorted to those little collapsible dollies. The next time you are strapped into your seat waiting for takeoff, count the number of people you can see from where you sit. Multiply that number by one hundred sixty pounds, add forty or fifty more pounds per passenger for luggage, and you'll have a (low) estimate of what the plane is being asked to carry.

The weight of the luggage is supported by a second floor, under which is the metal frame holding the plane together. Under that frame is another layer of thin metal skin. After you get to altitude and speed, the only thing under *that* layer of metal skin is thirty-five thousand feet of empty air.

Let's think about some *real* weight: the fuel. Depending on the model of the airplane, some of it might be stored under the seats or under the lavatories, but most of it is out there in the wings. Inside the DC10's three thousand, eight hundred sixty-one square feet of wing there can be as much as twenty-one thousand, seven hundred gallons of jet fuel. That's almost one hundred fifty *thousand* pounds hanging out there in space, attached to the fuselage at a right angle.

Back to the passengers. Depending upon the seating arrangement, your flight will be shared by anywhere from two hundred fifty-five to three hundred eighty souls. Each soul is housed in a body averaging one hundred sixty pounds. (And don't forget the overstuffed luggage down in the cargo hold.) The airline will be the first to admit it is "tricky" to figure out real and actual payload of any given flight, but the maximum is ninety-eight thousand-five hundred pounds.

I find myself more interested in yet another weight statistic. The DC10 we flew on to Alaska had a Maximum Takeoff Weight of four hundred fifty-five thousand pounds. More than that and it won't clear the end of the runway. It had a Maximum *Landing* Weight of three hundred sixty-three thousand pounds. More than that and it won't be able to stop in time. Perhaps tires will blow out or the landing gear will collapse. If you run these figures through the logic section of your brain, you realize that this flying pop can has to *lose* ninety-one thousand, five hundred pounds before it can safely land again. Fuel, obviously. If the flight is too short, something has to be left on the ground. Like extra fuel, for instance. Personally, I'm in favor of having extra fuel.

Now, let's presume we have correctly calculated the gross weight and our DC10 has made it off the ground. We rise to thirty-five thousand feet altitude. Our aluminum canister, bearing all the collective weight of fuel and folk and paraphernalia, is now holding up its own body, its engines, its fuel tanks, wheels, controls and hydraulics, and is also moving through the air at six hundred miles per hour. Hanging from the fuel-laden wings, which are held on with man-made bolts and rivets, the engines are roaring and vibrating and generating enough thrust to push this whole thing along, but without tearing themselves from their mountings.

Speaking of wings and engines, the DC10 driver's manual contains a few other choice statistics. The wings need to be moving at two hundred ten miles per hour before they can get the fuselage airborne. Three times as fast as you (should) drive on the interstate. Upon landing, the plane must hit the concrete going at *least* one hundred fifty miles per hour or else. "Yeah?" I hear you saying. "Or else what?" Or else the wings will "stall," which is a technical term for "quit flying." But the driver's manual contains an even more frightening number than Minimum Landing Speed. It is called the Never-Exceed Speed. On this plane the Never-Exceed Speed is .95 Mach. You do *not* want to go any faster (such as in a steep dive) and you don't want to know what will happen if you do.

Well. There I sat belted into my window seat, my right shoulder six inches from being outside, sitting on a strip of heavily laden metal thirty-five thousand feet in the air. Needless to say, if my imagination hadn't been numbed by the whole process I would not have been there. To get there, as Hemingway put it, I had to "suspend the functioning of imagination."

BRAVE NEW PAYLOAD

Loren Eiseley asked readers to contemplate a single question: Exactly *what* is so important about having big skulls and oversized brains? What justifies the evolutionary risk? Where we lack fangs we have the ability to imagine weapons. Where we lack strong legs we invent wheels. Lacking thick fur, we come up with central heating. We can even formulate an alphabet and thereby preserve our ideas for the benefit of future human beings.

Flying is the latest achievement of the human imagination, and I don't mean the creation of the DC10. I mean the ability we have developed to *suppress* our imagination, at will, in order to enjoy ourselves. Samuel Taylor Coleridge called it "the willing suspension of disbelief for the moment." If you don't want to examine a helicopter to see if it can fly, look at a roller coaster. Consider skydiving.

We have built up to it for generations, as can be seen in the example of the military. It has been recognized for years that when you put men into uniform clothing and make them walk in uniform formations and conform to uniform thinking, they will do things they would not do as individuals. They will shoot at complete strangers. They will run toward complete strangers who are shooting at *them*.

My generation was frightened by two books, George Orwell's *1984* and Aldous Huxley's *Brave New World*. Both present scenarios in which human imagination is systematically and deliberately bred out of the species. In an Orwellian airplane terminal, we would be zombies wandering through mazes of intersecting concourses staring at "Arrival" and "Departure" monitors, unable to recognize or remember anyone else in the crowd, unable even to remember our flight number.

And speaking of books, it is unusual to see anyone reading real literature in an airport terminal. The place lends itself more to thrillers and romance and popularized history. It is even more unusual to see real works of art in an airport. Nor do you hear classical music. Fine paintings, beautiful sculptures and recognizable music would be too distinctive, too much of a reminder of individualism. Art and music also stimulate the emotions. If you're going flying, better stick to those weekly news magazines and elevator music.

The irony of an airport's lack of individualistic art hits you when you consider how many people in airports are either coming from or going toward emotional experiences. Weddings, reunions, funerals, business deals. Going to visit newborns, going to visit the sick. Going on honeymoons or anniversary trips, going to see exciting new places or to revisit cherished old ones. Some passengers are arriving in this country for the very first time and are experiencing slight culture shock. Of all the places we go where we would appreciate a little Monet or Mozart, a bit of Bach or Sargent, an airport terminal must be near the top of the list.

Yet the terminal ruthlessly stifles all feeling. Passengers who have just "deplaned" walk the long concourse, passing identical magazine stands selling identical merchandise, looking at "Arrival" monitors that are no longer relevant, looking out windows at identical airplanes being loaded from identical waiting areas. Their eyes seek the carpet, only looking up for signs to direct them to their luggage.

Dozens have impulsively punched numbers into their cell phones, hoping to hear a familiar voice. They proceed to the luggage place where they stand and stare at strangers' bags going around and around, but do not look at the strangers. They retrieve their bags, check the tags because their bags look so much like all the others, and walk out of the building. Once outside, they blink and frown and look around squinting. They look at the sky curiously as if they have just awakened from a dream.

In the future, human imagination will no doubt invent other ways to move even more people at higher speeds and with greater efficiency across longer distances. In fact, it has already been imagined. In the old television series called *Star Trek* the spaceship was equipped with a transporter device. Bodies and souls entered a sterile-looking chamber where they were transformed into shimmery blobs of disoriented electrons to zip around in empty space until being reconstituted in an identical chamber somewhere else.

BACK IN TOUCH

The airport and the airplane ride may have been routine, but we found Kodiak Island was everything but. A couple of days after we arrived, my son's friend invited us to try ocean kayaking. Paddling my solo kayak into the misty corridor between Kodiak and a smaller island, I heard a roar and saw a floatplane coming right at me as it took off. It became airborne so close to my kayak that I could have counted its rivets. The next day we went out onto the docks to look at the fishing boats, where we were warned to keep an eye out for sea lions. They had been known to leap onto the docks and attack people. We took a hike through the dense woods, where there was a chance of having a Kodiak bear chase us. And if a bear did chase us and we ran into the woods, we would probably run straight into thickets of poisonous devil's club.

A Russian sailor from a three-masted sailing ship offered to give us a private tour of the crew's sleeping quarters, but he was really out to sell us contraband souvenirs. Not a day went by that you could call ordinary.

The day we were to leave Kodiak dawned to a cold gray drizzle. Packing my bag, I looked out the window toward the Sitka spruce trees. Less than ten yards from the house, they were invisible except for the dripping branches protruding out of the fog. My Pre-Flight Worry function clicked on, of course, but somehow our stay in Kodiak seemed to have rendered it rather sluggish. I just couldn't work up a decent state of nerves that morning. Like any good paranoid, I *knew* what to worry about. If we missed the Kodiak-to-Anchorage plane, or if weather grounded it, we'd then miss the once-a-week charter flight to Denver. At that point we would have to choose between spending lots of money changing to a regular airline and spending lots of time waiting for the next charter plane. Should we plan to stay in Anchorage, or stay in Kodiak? As worry material goes, it was prime.

Strange to say, I just couldn't seem to get too worried about any of it.

When I phoned the airport to ask whether there would be a flight that day, the lady on the phone said the plane from Anchorage *might* take a chance on the weather and it *might* even find a hole in the overcast and be able to land once it got to Kodiak. So we put on our ponchos and sloshed out to the car with our bags. On Kodiak Island there is no interstate highway to take you to the airport. We drove the three miles dodging deep potholes, holding our breath as we passed the factory where fish are made into cat food, watched for deer and bears and mudslides on the pavement, and watched for places where there is no pavement at all.

There is no outlying parking at Kodiak airport. There isn't a concourse, either. Our host parked in front of the little building and we went in. We joined about twenty other people, all Anchorage-bound passengers and their friends and relatives who'd come to see them off. We were dripping wet, we were carrying our own luggage, and we were crowded into a waiting area that in a big international airport would have been a restroom. A nice young man checked our heavier bags for us and set them on a cart that he would push out to the plane, if the plane arrived. He told us to help ourselves to the coffee.

The coffee was strong and fresh and it was free. You just poured however much you wanted from a glass pot. People stood around drinking it and talking. They were making jokes about the weather, talking about sports and fishing, exchanging opinions about inflation and foreign policy and showing off their souvenir T-shirts. And, of course, souvenir caps.

Me, I stood at the rain-streaked window with my coffee. Somebody had to worry about the condition of the runway, and I seemed like the only person who cared enough to do it. But my heart wasn't in it. Anyway, the far side of the runway was hidden in the fog. I did manage a few glimpses of the centerline whenever a hard gust of wind sent the sheets of rain slanting over the pavement. The Aircraft Owners and Pilots Association (AOPA) has an airport directory called *Aviation USA* and it says Kodiak has "three runways: longest, 7,548 feet long, 150 feet wide." This can be compared with the old abandoned airstrip at Denver's former airport: it was 12,000 feet long and 200 feet wide.

And the old one at Denver was concrete. Kodiak's was asphalt. Kodiak's weather wreaks havoc with asphalt.

Aviation USA's report on Kodiak's airport goes on to say, "Obstructions include mountains N, S & W; birds and deer in vicinity. Standing water first 1000 feet of Runway 18 during rainy periods." Well, I could *see* the standing water. And I could also visualize a passenger jet descending toward it, weaving between 2000-foot mountains in wind gusts to land on it. I could imagine the pilot staring out through a wet, opaque windshield while approaching a flooded airstrip at over a hundred miles per hour. I not only began to feel like I did not want to get on the plane, I was pretty nervous about standing there in the terminal.

My worry hot-button began to glow warmly. I thought, what's the minimum landing speed of a partly loaded 737? I thought, why is that a question?

A sudden stir of conversation going through the crowd made me turn around. A big bearded fellow in a smelly plaid shirt told me the 737 had just taken off from Anchorage. It would be circling Kodiak in fifty-five minutes. People received the news with smiles and went back to their conversations. I started toward the two-person restroom at the other end of the building, but on the way got interested in the décor. Among the embellishments was a stuffed Kodiak bear that someone had donated to cheer

The Terminal Imagination

up the place. The animal stood on his hind legs, eight feet tall with three-inch teeth and claws.

The walls behind the bear were decorated with calendars and posters, maps of Alaska and photos of floatplanes and wildlife. There was also a bulletin board with a collection of hand-lettered ads thumbtacked to it. "Fishing Boat Needs Experienced Crew. Baltic Sea, out ten weeks." Or "Custom Smoking, Venison or Salmon." Or my favorite, "For Sale: Winch and Chain Saw. Will Trade for A Washer/Dryer or A Good Rifle. Call Betty."

The room was filled with the odor of wet wool shirts and damp denim, not to mention the almost toxic signature scent of plastic rain gear. It mingled with a whiff of fish from sportsmen going home with their salmon packed in picnic coolers. Anywhere near the coffeepot the temperature was like a sauna, while next to the doorway it was more like an igloo.

Another announcement came over the radio and was transmitted from passenger to passenger. The Anchorage pilot was now circling Kodiak and talking to the agent at the airline desk. She kept listening and shrugging her shoulders. Someone stuck his head out the door to see if the weather was clearing any. The pilot had to make a decision: to land or not to land? Try it now or try again tomorrow?

Most of us had schedules waiting for us. We needed to get back to the land of cell phones and antacid tablets. But no one seemed concerned about it. Conversations continued, smiles stayed in place, and no one whined about the weather, the airline, the schedules or anything else. I thought about the Denver airport. There I had once seen a man turn red and scream at a ticket agent because he *had* to get on a certain flight and could *not* wait around for the one that would take off twenty minutes later.

Fifteen minutes passed. The news on the terminal grapevine was that the pilot was still circling up there, waiting for the wind to blow a hole in the clouds that enveloped the island.

I got a fresh cup of coffee and went back to the window. I thought the fog had lifted a little. I thought I could almost see the other side of the runway. And then I saw the dim form of something coming toward me out of the mist. Then, as if two curtains made of rain had suddenly opened, there was a gleaming MarkAir 737 rushing at the terminal, weaving and skidding and throwing up high rooster tails of water over its tail. On it came, decelerating at an almost unbelievable rate until it slid to a stop just outside the window. The crowd cheered and applauded; the copilot opened her little side window and waved and grinned.

The Terminal Imagination

I dashed for the restroom. "Too much coffee?" asked the stranger next to me at the urinals. "Yes," I said. "Same here," he said. "Happens to me every week."

There's no air-conditioned loading tunnel at Kodiak, no hiding from the fact that you are boarding an airplane in a chilly driving rain. We waded through water, ankle deep, and stood in water waiting our turn to climb the steep boarding steps. The jet engine on the far side of the plane was still running. The one next to us was just spinning with a whirring noise like a big fan. I could smell the exhaust. I could feel the heat waves coming off the engine, and when I took hold of the rails on the steps I could feel the vibration. There was nothing numb and zombielike about *this* loading process.

The flight attendant slammed the door right behind us and the plane began to roll almost before we got to our seats. I fell down into mine and grabbed for the lap belt. Looking out the window was like looking into a washing machine someone had filled with clam chowder. But oddly enough, I wasn't worried about takeoff. I discovered I was almost eager to see what it would be like. I was no longer hesitant to take to the thin air in a flying tin can. I was more fearful of becoming a zombie, of having my senses dulled. Of losing imagination.

Sameness and uniformity are our modern opiates. What I was feeling during that takeoff was awareness. I was aware of the screaming of the engines as they clawed upward toward open air. I was aware of the fuel-filled heavy wings flexing and yawing in the air pockets and hard gusts of wind. I felt the reality of it. It was unvarnished, unpretentious, life-in-your-face reality.

We held hands during takeoff. After the plane leveled off in smooth air, Sharon took out her book. "Did you bring something to read on the plane?" she asked.

"Eiseley," I replied. "I need to finish *The Immense Journey.*"

With a little imagination, what a journey it can be.

INTRODUCTION TO *Following Where the River Begins*

Although I make my living as a teacher and scholar, this is not a scholarly work. It is not about history, or geology, or psychology, or the social relationship between professors and pupils. This is a journey through one man's inner landscape, a ramble from the valleys where the shadow of doubt seems perpetual to the heights that seem, like the mountains, to be imperceptibly shrinking each year.

My aim is only domestic and purely private, as Montaigne wrote when he penned the first specimens of the essay genre. Montaigne offered his to his relatives and friends so that, when they had lost him, they might "recognize in my essays some characteristics of my habits and humors, and thus have a way to keep their knowledge of me more complete, more alive."

To those who know me and those who do not, I offer this essay along with a professorial admonition: go and find your headwaters, but do not dwell in them; anticipate confluences, and rejoice in them; and wherever you are on the river, make that your river of most moment.

Following Where the River Begins

PART ONE • THE FIRST DAY OF CLASS

Glacier Basin Campground, Rocky Mountain National Park, Colorado. Perhaps I'm just anxious to get into more remote wilderness, perhaps I have just seen too many of these government-operated complexes, or perhaps I am experiencing that old familiar first-day-of-class cynicism; whatever the cause, I don't feel particularly thrilled to be here. A system of tidy gravel streets divides the meadow and forest into one hundred and fifty-two individual, family and group "sites." When you drive in, you do not need to set foot on the ground. You just roll down your window and tell the seasonal "ranger" that you made a reservation through Ticketron; from his window he hands you a map and a brochure and you are on your way to your site.

Loop B (One Way), Site 12 (Groups Only). Sitting in proper predetermined optimal locations you will find your dining table and your cooking grill, anchored in concrete. The choice of where to pitch your tent is up to you. This is a tent site area. Recreational vehicles have their own site area elsewhere and must park where the recreation engineers have decided that they must park. They must park in exactly the same place as every other RV before them. But with your tent you have a choice, and you will choose the level, rectangular spot, the place where the pine needles and pebbles have been swept away by hundreds of tent-pitchers who have slept there before you.

Your site is also within sight of the restroom, with its flush toilets (Please Do Not Wash Dishes Here). Every site, as a matter of fact and considerate federal planning, is in view of the restroom. No site is slighted. When I was a mere lad among these mountains, we called them "outhouses," or something more graphic but less euphonic; but when they have running water and flush toilets and skylights and ventilation fans, they deserve the filling station—excuse me, the "service" station—designation: restroom. There are even photosensitive cells to turn on the lights at dusk and snap them off again at dawn; the National Park Service determines the minimum amount of daylight needed to define "sunrise."

You may stroll on the trails here, or walk the campground's gravel streets and inspect all the other tents and recreational vehicles. Perhaps you would rather get a group together for a turf-ripping game of volleyball or football. Your playing field is a delicate glacial meadow; it is like the oval arena of an enormous coliseum, and the stadium wall is a million-year-old moraine.

You may listen to an evening lecturer deliver a canned all-audience, all-purpose, nonpromotional slide talk at the rustic amphitheater; or you might want to just kick back and listen to some music. Well, it is actually cassette cacophony in stereo, emanating from Group Site Number 11 (tonight featuring a nasal engagement with Willie Nelson and live accompaniment—a spoon drumming a garbage can, and someone trying to beat out a bongo rhythm on a picnic table). If Willie's wailin' doesn't fit your musical taste, tune in to Group Site Number 12 instead, where the tape player is presenting low-fidelity punk rock accompanied by a live percussion section of Dubble Bubble.

It occurs to me that if all the Walkmen and stereophones and Hitachis were ever to get together and agree on a single pitch and a common rhythm, that whole vast moraine wall out there might, like Jericho's, come tumbling down. What would we do if that immense range of rock began to roll down through the meadows? Jump into our vehicles, of course, limber up the cameras and videocams, and drive closer. A traffic jam of shutter-snappers would soon block the path of the avalanche. Kodacolor kamikazes. Charge into that photo opportunity! Damn the light values! I have not yet begun to compose my shot! Do I exaggerate? Have *you* ever seen a tourist with an Instamatic shooting a picture of a deer that is standing at least three hundred yards away? Or the guy with the 500 mm lens who is walking up to a bull elk in rutting season?

Climb any hill where you can take a peek over that high moraine of unstable stone and you will discover another picture: the topless granite pyramids of the Rocky Mountains beyond, unseen from the campground. The Winnebago trekkers are confronted by that stern mass unexpectedly, as they round the end of the moraine; they stomp the gas pedal and hurry like little hard-shell insects to get up the Front Range passes, through the shadowed canyons, and back out into the safe, flat, open country beyond. Their haste will be silent and careful, like Hannibal's legions quietly sneaking through the looming Alps.

But the Winnebagos and Sportsmen, the Airstreams and Good Sams will not be under way until morning. Right now, their doors are closed and the cold blue-gray glow of television sets can be seen at the windows. It is near twilight. The restroom lights will soon come on. The moon may come up. Stars may come out. The evening interpretive program will definitely be held.

And now the sun slides down atop the Front Range, glissades along one shoulder of Longs Peak. Incredible intensities of light, the kind that happen just before sunset, make brilliant corridors through the forest. Streaks of light, nearly horizontal, shine past stone spires, through narrow aisles in the trees. Bright stripes and long shadows cut across the wide moraine meadow. This day's final sunbeams, thin and pale, sneak between the trees to infiltrate our camp. They become a backlight for wisps of smoke rising from my after-coffee cigar.

This is a camp of youth, here on the lap of the Front Range. Broad and level before me, a green gleam in that last ray of sun, the oldest moraine park in the Rocky Mountains takes its evening rest, free of those millions of tons of ice that formed it. But why is it, I wonder, that I sit here remembering the ice? From some primordial corner of my subconscious there has come a dread of that ancient perpetual cold. I feel it when the night breezes come off the Continental Divide carrying that chilly scent of old icepacks and snow. Once at a lake well below timberline, in a month well into summer, my wife and I paused in our evening walk; a change in the wind, hardly noticeable, introduced a new smell to the pine forest. We looked at each other. "Snow," we said, and stood there sniffing at the air with flared nostrils, like a couple of Neanderthals. Tonight there is a teasing, fleeting hint of that same old smell. But the ice age is gone, and it is as if this open park will never again be under the burden of glaciers.

At our group site, young people are strumming guitars, glad to be free of whatever ancient pressures have formed *them*. "Abilene" is the song this evening. Folks down there don't treat you mean, in Abilene. Where, none of them seems curious to know, *is* Abilene?

That much, at least, seems consistent. They are not curious about anything, as far as I can tell. Perhaps if they were from flatland farms, or from small towns, they would be more intrigued by these new surroundings. But they are from urban centers where life is restless, always moving from one surrounding to another. They "watch" music on videos, their finger on the remote control button ready to change channels. They spend hours aimlessly cruising in cars, looking for each other. They gather in the mall. If they find themselves alone, they reach out to touch—anyone—on the telephone. When they find themselves away from malls and cars and television, where they could make their own solo discoveries on a Rocky Mountain moraine, their reaction is to avoid being curious about it. Instead, they stay clustered together near the camp and near the bus. The problem is that they will do the same thing intellectually when we get down to our lessons. If they have curiosity, I can teach them; if they do not have curiosity, I can only occupy their time.

For the sake of a little distance, or perhaps for the sake of a little symbolism, I remove myself further from the guitar crowd. I assume my pose, my attitude of contemplation. My seat is a patch of meadow located between the ancient mountain moraine and the recent youths—a bit closer to the youths than to the mountains, I am amused to notice.

From here, I can look them over. From here, some of them begin to look less like urbanites and more like individuals. But they are still strange individuals. One kid's haircut looks like a wig made out of used pipe cleaners; another student is wearing enough leather and chains to harness a team of carriage horses. They appear to be crying out for attention, but they are actually mainstream residents of large cities, just ordinary youngsters trying to look like somebody. Somebody on MTV, most likely. What the heck: I used to try to look like Roy Rogers.

Not one of them wants to walk over here and start a discussion with me; I don't see one of them that I would walk over to talk to, either. It's a bad sign for a teacher to resent having students nearby, a sign of impending "burnout." Maybe I need a sabbatical. Maybe I should get into some other business. What would Roy Rogers do?

It is a welcome evening, at least. As soon as the sun is gone, the mountain cold drops down on us as if someone opened a freezer door. It was a relief to get out of the big bus and out into some air that was not "conditioned." We spent the day driving from our Colorado Springs campus to this campground on the east side of Rocky Mountain National Park. It would be more accurate to say that we were driven: Harold is the ex-army driver of the college's venerable bus, a Trailways castoff. Sitting behind Harold, we hurtled north along the interstate highway and amid the foothills to Denver, then through the city's Chinese-puzzle traffic routes and out into the farm country, then turned west into the valleys of the foothills, heading for Big Thompson Canyon.

Along this route into the Rockies, the first sign of the mountains comes in the form of a long hogback sliced in half where the highway engineers excavated their right-of-way. It is known locally as Devil's Backbone, a name that is very accurate. In a process of unimaginable duration, an ancient seafloor of lime-rich sediment rose more than a mile above the level of the sea. Hardened into rock, this section tilted and tilted until the old sedimentary layers were vertical. Wind, rain, frost, and tremblings of the earth then carved it into a shape resembling the vertebrae of some incredible monster—or demon.

The highway zips through the man-made gap in the Backbone, follows the level floodplain for a few miles, then starts to climb again, up around the shoulder of a sandstone uplift, and then drops down once again to cross a troughlike little valley. On the far side of this valley, the slopes become steeper. The highway has to turn and head into a natural cut in the slope, a gap between the cuestas. On the other side is Triassic Lyons Sandstone—bright pink. Further on, the stone becomes brick red: the Pennsylvania formation, 135 million years old. Roughly.

Joe Gordon, the institute director, turns on the speaker system and hands me the microphone. Through a gap in the cuesta, the bus rolls on over the Triassic, picks up speed, and zips down the Pennsylvania formation. Directly ahead is the *really* old stuff: Precambrian granite. How long ago was it?—a billion years, perhaps?—this gray wall in front of us was molten, a thick liquid layer oozing over older layers, building a thicker mass, trapping crystals in itself, making weird shapes like folded cloth that would be there when it cooled, becoming denser and denser.

Harold aims the bus at the Narrows. It is a V-shaped gouge, barely wide enough for both the highway and the river. In 1976, it proved wide enough only for the river. Overnight, the highway was gone. In a single weekend, one hundred and forty-five people died here, my brother put himself at risk in order to save others, and I had one of the stranger experiences of my life. Joe wants me to tell the students how the Big Flood scoured a wide, two-lane asphalt highway—*this* highway—completely out of the canyon. Joe can be a sadistic son-of-a-gun at times, and this is one of those times. Here we are, trapped in a steel casket on wheels, heading up the river into that deep slit where more than a hundred people died, and he wants these kids to hear all the details.

It's not often that I get an atmosphere like this for my lectures: the walls of the Narrows are grim and gray today, seeming to hold the pavement prisoner. Even in sunshine, this drab gray stone feels oppressive. With overcast sitting overhead like a lid, it seems almost malevolent. In Major Powell's Grand Canyon diary, written during his exploration in 1869, the scientific-sounding tone changed to pessimism and gloom each time his tiny group entered walls of granite. When the boats were plunging down-river between walls of marble or sandstone or even lava, the group took heart; each time they ran back into the granite, the strange depression set in again. Here in the Narrows of the Thompson, I feel hints of the same dread.

The river today is a boiling brown soup of spring runoff, and dark storm clouds make a roof over the granite slit. In 1976, some even darker clouds formed over the upper canyon. It was during the late afternoon and evening of July 31, a Saturday; unusually large masses of moist air arrived, and equally unusual was that they came from both the Pacific Ocean and the Gulf of Mexico. Adding to the potential for disaster, a Canadian cold front arrived on that same day, which was also out of the ordinary. The moist masses and the cold masses met, directly above the Thompson River watershed. There they mixed, and the mixture began to rise like bread dough. The wet air went straight up, climbing until it had formed a soggy thunderhead more than sixty thousand feet high.

There was one more odd thing about that Saturday's weather. The wind was blowing lightly from the east, holding the moisture against the Rockies. In the winter, this would be an indication that a heavy snowstorm was coming. The saturated, stationary thunderhead hovered over the Thompson drainage, gathering more and more moisture, becoming an airborne reservoir sixty-two thousand feet deep. And then . . . it let go. In Colorado, the average annual rainfall is roughly twelve inches. "And last year," a state joke goes, "we got our twelve inches on August 5." On this July 31, it was no joke. In the four hours between 6:30 and 10:30 P.M., twelve inches of rain came down. More followed. Much more.

Back to our geology lesson. The highway enters the mountains by way of the Narrows, a V-shaped slit in the granite. If the ancient glaciers had flowed through here, I explained to the students, these "narrows" would be

U-shaped instead. They would be wider and straighter, more like a long valley smoothed out by glacial grinders of ice and rock. Up where the July 31 thunderburst came to earth, the narrows open out into just such a valley. Up there, the ancient ice and subsequent erosion have created flat gravel "parks" with very little soil in them to absorb water. They are veined by a system of wide, shallow drainages.

The flat parks and the U-shaped canyons gathered up the deluge. When the resulting wall of water got to the narrow, V-shaped part, it was twenty feet high. It made kindling out of cabins, motels, wayside businesses; it took automobiles and trucks and tossed them in a churn with boulders ten and twenty feet thick, hurling the whole muddy, deafening mass out onto the flat land between the cuestas and the hogback. It ground up the highway, with all of the asphalt and all the fill rock, and washed it away like sand. It scoured the whole canyon clean. It killed 145 human beings, some of whom were found miles beyond the mouth of the Narrows. Six were never found at all.

I point out the high-water mark to the students. It is hard to see from a bus, because in the narrower stretches it is thirty or forty feet up on the wall. I tell tales of seeing twisted, unrecognizable debris that used to be homes and fences, cars and utility poles; I talk about the dozens and dozens of battered, sodden bodies that came down on the flood. I relate accounts of people who were trapped in absolute blackness with the rain and the flood howling in a maelstrom around their cabins; I tell how some people clung all night to steep hillsides where they had climbed to safety, there to tremble in the dark with that inescapable roar all around them, punctuated by the unearthly sound of huge granite boulders thudding together in the water. Often, somewhere below in the blackness, they would hear propane storage tanks floating the flood, hissing and banging. They could smell the gas. Some heard victims calling for help, never to be heard again.

Our students watch the canyon walls go by, staring through the tinted bus windows with indifferent detachment. Joe looks at them, looks at me, and shrugs. We have a long way to go.

I slouch back into my seat, more depressed by these students than I am by the gray walls of stone. My thoughts are focused on the flood, reliving the story I did *not* tell. At the time, riding up in the bus toward the antiseptic campground, the story seemed unrelated to this group. But later, down near the Colorado River, it would take on a spooky significance.

I have to begin by saying that my older brother and I have always led lives whose courses rarely intersect. If I saw myself as Roy Rogers, I usually cast him in the role of John Wayne. While I got along well with our high school teachers, Al seemed to live under the constant threat of suspension from school. He went to Alaska; I went to college. I became a professional student; he became a union electrician and businessman. While I was driving a Volkswagen bus and wearing a beard, he drove a Jeep and became captain of the sheriff's four-wheel-drive posse.

In 1976 he was living up in Estes Park. I was living in Fort Collins, forty-five miles away. On July 31, that fateful Saturday afternoon, a light rain was falling in Fort Collins and I heard on the 5:00 news that a "stationary front" and "rain cells" of unusual size were hanging over the eastern slope of the Rockies. On the late-night news, I heard the first fragmentary reports of a flood in the canyon. None of the newspeople seemed to know what was actually going on, other than that the state patrol had closed the canyon and that the telephone lines were down. But by that time, one victim of the flood was already a dead man: State Patrol Sergeant Hugh Purdy, driving up the flooded canyon to assess the situation before sending his men into it, had been trapped and drowned. Others were dying. Volunteer rescue groups, including the sheriff's four-wheel-drive patrol, were being assembled. I went to bed and slept, but woke up several times during the night with the peculiar feeling that someone had been talking to me, there in the room. Each time I awoke, I lay there expecting the phone to ring. I did not know why it *should* ring, but I had the feeling that it would.

On Sunday morning, the size of the disaster was becoming apparent. I ate my breakfast, read my newspapers, and started to go about my Sunday routine. Something still bothered me, and I could only pace the house. Somebody, I felt, was trying to call me.

I tried the telephone several times but could not reach either my parents or my brother. The lines were all down to Estes Park, but radio operators had assured the media that all was well in Estes. No flood damage up there. There were rumors of damage to the dam, below town, but no danger to residents upstream. Somehow I wasn't reassured, and the feeling persisted that somebody was trying to call me.

I told my wife that I was going downtown. As I drove, this odd "signal" became stronger. Two realizations hit me simultaneously, right at the intersection of Shields Street and Mulberry Avenue. First, I suddenly knew without a shadow of a doubt that it was Al who was trying to contact me.

Second, I knew that I had to drive to the Fort Collins sheriff's office. On Sunday? With a county emergency going on?

I don't remember much about the deputy I found on duty, except that he, too, was worried. Yes, he had met Al on a few occasions but didn't know him too well. Yes, he imagined the patrol was out in the canyon. No, the radio contact was poor, and no personal messages were being sent. Between the various state emergency groups and the national guard and ham operators, the radio frequencies were jammed. He hadn't heard any messages about the patrol, but there might have been some.

At this point I still knew next to nothing about the details of the flood; logically, I should have gone home and let the matter drop. But that "call" was still coming through. I walked around the desk and put my finger on the big county map above the dispatcher's desk.

"Look," I said, "I've been all over those hills around the Big Thompson Canyon. The highway is gone" (how did I know that?), "but a guy with a Jeep could go clear over to the Carter Lake road, up the Pole Hill road, and . . . right here . . . drop into the canyon. There's an old access road there. And another one up here, by Waltonia. I can do it. If it's open, I can guide some rescue guys in there."

I pleaded with the deputy. I argued. I begged for a four-wheel-drive, anything. I would borrow one somewhere. I could help.

What I wasn't telling him was that my whole head, even my guts, were being twisted up like dry rawhide knots. Al needed me, and I didn't know why.

In the end, the deputy persuaded me to just go home. He took my number, in case the sheriff could use me, but told me the best thing to do was to wait and see. They had plenty of help. More would just be in the way. So I went home and puttered around in my workshop, my mind still registering my brother's need to get in touch with me. There in the workshop, it seemed a good idea to get my carbiners and piton hammer together and put them in my pack.

I never did get up the canyon, not until a week had gone by and we drove up by the longer route to see my parents. And that was when I learned that my brother had been a hero of the flood. Responding to the mobilization call, he and Jim Graffe had climbed into his Jeep and started down the canyon in a heavy downpour. Their job was to warn residents to evacuate. The river was already churning, but the main surge was yet to come.

Not far into the canyon, at about 7:00 P.M., the two men spotted a cabin afloat in the river; it had jammed up against some rocks on the opposite side, but could drift off again as the water continued to rise. They could see two women inside, the younger one waving hysterically toward the beam of the Jeep's headlights. Lacking ropes, Al and Jim commandeered a nylon clothesline, tied one end to the bumper, and waded through the chest-high water to secure the other end to the cabin porch. Jim was hit by a floating tree and knocked off his feet, but recovered. They worked together to bring back first one woman, then the other, trusting their lives to that fragile rope and hoping that the cabin would not shift again before they got back to the Jeep. In recognition of this act, the men were awarded lifesaving certificates.

Later, further downcanyon, my brother had to watch as two people drove off the eroding highway and into the floodwaters, never to be seen alive again.

The posse worked all through the evening and into the night, searching for survivors, seeing bodies that they could not recover. Finally, they were trapped. All the routes of escape were washed out or blocked by landslides, and Al found himself in charge of thirty wet, frightened people. The water rose. The Jeeps were no longer safe. Reluctantly, he directed the caravan to the last bit of solid ground where the water was only up to the axles and ordered the group to abandon the vehicles. As they struggled up the steep, soggy mountainside in pitch blackness, Al made a last radio report to the dispatcher. He was more than half convinced that his own death was waiting out there in the dark, and his mind was full of final thoughts of home and family. His frightened wife overheard that radio message, saying that they were abandoning the Jeeps. Moments later, my wakeful night began.

The bus growls over the last hill, and we get our first view of the Estes Park valley with Longs Peak standing sentinel in the background. Everything looks peaceful and still. The clouds have broken, and those blue Colorado skies are opening up for us. Joe hands me the microphone.

"Want to tell them the history of Estes Park?" he says.

"Not particularly," I reply.

ಌ

The cigar burns short and goes out. My eye happens to fall on a dim blur of blue tent that I can see over there at the edge of the trees. My tent.

Evening air chills my neck and arms. An overpowering urge suddenly hits me, a desire to get my shivering body undressed and into my bedroll. But not to sleep. I want the feeling of solitude I get when that thin fabric is surrounding me, keeping warmth and sounds inside, and I want my little metal jigger of brandy warmed over my candle lantern. I want pillow talk in a sleeping bag.

That same night breeze that is putting goosebumps on my arms is also brushing the treetops and talking to the moraine and meadow. In five minutes, the very last bit of dim light will be gone. It will be too dark to write in my journal—but writing pages in a journal is the nearest thing to pillow talk that I have tonight. I could go on writing, in the tent, with the candle lantern; but if I go into the tent, I will have to face the fact that she is not there, and in my present mood I do not want to admit that. So, instead, I walk toward the campfire, thinking of another time, of a high-country camp where she and I were alone. It's finally time to join the students and the singing and the guitars.

PART TWO • THE CONTINENTAL DIVIDE

The music of the evening guitars becomes softer and the tunes become more mellow, and one by one our campers rise and drift off in the direction of their tents. This pattern, at least, is the same every year. The harsh music is silenced; the loud laughter and smart remarks subside as the night grows darker, deeper and colder. The last few students who stay up are grouped close together, speaking in muted voices. Then they too are gone, and the black night is full of silence.

Within the space of an eye-flick, it seems, it's morning again.

Most of the year, I sleep indoors and find each morning duplicating the one before it. Each morning I rise and wash the sleep from my eyes, then wander toward the kitchen. Going past the door to the den, I see my desk and the ungraded papers from the night before, next to the pile of unanswered letters, next to a crusty coffee cup. In the kitchen, the cat is usually waiting for me to open the back door. She knows the routine. Night came and went while I slept, and I have once again awakened without even noticing that nothing has changed. It doesn't occur to me even to think about it. Everything is just as it was, and the new day of life starts with a comfortable sameness. It is not particularly interesting, but it is comfortable.

Sleeping out of doors, however, whether in the mountains or out on the tallgrass prairie, I always wake up with the feeling that the morning has taken me by surprise. Some mornings I am almost amazed to find myself there. Somewhere during the night, during those six or eight hours of my unconsciousness, the mountains seemed to go away into the blackness, or the rim of the prairie melted into darkness; when I first open my eyes in that sweet early dazzle of day, the landscape seems to rush back to me again.

The feeling reminds me of being at the ocean on a morning when the fog is low and thick, and all I see of that vast ocean is the narrow band of water lapping the sand at my feet—and then the fog burns off and vanishes, and I stand transfixed by the sight of all that ocean stretching toward a boundless horizon. It was always there; yet somehow in the fog it was *not* there.

And here on the front range of the Rocky Mountains, on the first morning of my trip with these students, it has happened again. Through the open flap of my tent I see the mountains, which have just now returned from some nighttime chamber, fresh green under a columbine-colored sky. They seem brand new, ages old. The air is fresh and new and cold, and there is no breeze at all. Today something new will begin, I think, because yesterday's world went away with the twilight mountains and this morning the mountains have returned without it.

I pull on my pants and shirt and windbreaker, drag my sleeping bag out of the tent and lay it open to the dry, fresh air, and then I stroll toward the breakfast table.

Breakfast is student-group style, which means grabbing anything within reach, shoving it into the mouth as fast as possible, and grabbing for more. More than a dozen people crowd toward one end of the table, snatching what they can. The student trio responsible for arranging today's meals has decided to fix breakfast by simply opening the food lockers and yelling, "Breakfast!" The effect is similar to what it would be if the city zoo decided to feed the animals by dumping all the food in the middle of the park and opening the cages.

Hands shoot out and grab oranges, apples, cans of juice; they snatch milk cartons, cereal packets, instant coffee. Above the din of this feeding frenzy I hear individuals demanding to know why they can't find plates or utensils: obviously they ignored our list of required personal equipment. Some cannot wait for the water to boil, or are afraid that someone will beat them to it if they do, so there is a rush to pour it lukewarm onto the instant oatmeal and powdered coffee.

I stand at the back of the mob, arms folded, holding my tin cup and aluminum plate. Gradually, the students drift away with full hands. None has taken notice of me. Not one has thought to say, "Oh, professor. Please, go ahead. Can I get you anything?" No respect for rank or age. So, I think as I stand there watching and waiting, this is the way we shall play the game this trip. I can insist that they treat me with deference; I can demand some respect and I will get it—as long as I am face-to-face with them. Or I can become part of their group—a buddy, a pal, a good guy. Or I can accept the real challenge and earn some respect for myself.

Finally, the herd has its food and has dispersed. Among the wreckage I manage to fill my Sierra cup with dry shredded wheat cubes and find a bruised banana. I walk away from camp to break my fast in peace.

As I sit on my rock, munching dry cereal, I begin to brood. I've made a serious mistake in not bringing my own cooking outfit and some food. Perhaps in some town along our way I can stop and buy some basic survival munchies for myself, so I won't have to deal with these mass-meal situations and a bunch of rude adolescents. "Next trip," my notebook says, "bring backpack stove, coffee, hard fruit and gorp. Bring cheese, brandy and crackers." *"Someone* you go camping with," my small interior voice says, "has spoiled you, hasn't she?"

There is a heady aroma of fresh, real coffee coming from the group camp across the road. I wander over there, pretending that I am in search of a water spigot. Unlike ours, this camp is a model of efficiency. There are two portable kitchen boxes on legs; next to them, two gas stoves hiss under coffeepots, and frying pans sizzle under scrambled eggs and pancakes. This seems to be a group of young women—either scouts or a church group, I suspect. One young lady nods politely at me and smiles. This is what I should be doing, I think to myself, teaching some sort of disciplined group. I always envy my friends who teach at the Air Force Academy, with their students who march in ranks, never miss class, and say "Sir!" to every suggestion. Various officers who teach at the academy have told me that it is not like that at all, but still I cling to the fantasy of a truly respectful student body. It's the "Mr. Chips Syndrome," a classic foreshadowing of professorial burnout.

In spite of the young lady's friendly smile and my own despicable longings, I find I have too much pride to beg for a cup of coffee and a pancake. Instead, I slouch back past Frenzy Foods, swipe an orange, and go to my brooding-rock. West of here, the mountains wait. From these mountains flows the river of my childhood and of my youth. How different were the mornings then! I would sit in a warm kitchen, gorging on Mother's pancakes or waffles or scrambled eggs and bacon, looking through the window and down the hill at the river. Sometimes a trout would rise, and breakfast would be forgotten. I had to sit still and eat everything that had been set before me, but in my boy-spirit I was already outside, running to be there before the trout-ripple faded downstream.

*

Today we are going to where that little mountain river takes its head; we are going to drive Up Top. "Up top" is a common colloquialism in western mountain towns. Almost every town in the mountains has a highway leading to a pass, or to a mountaintop, and when someone says he spent the day "up top," that's where he was. My hometown's "up top" is the twelve thousand–foot summit of Trail Ridge, a road two miles high where you can find the clearest atmosphere on this continent.

Three routes cross Trail Ridge, none of which could be built in today's West. First, there is the faint remnant of the old Ute Trail, a migratory route predating the appearance of Europeans in the region. Somewhere in long-distant ages, even the Ute Trail was once a new concept, an idea in the mind of some primitive leader. But such trails will be seen no more. If a contemporary group of Native Americans set out to walk across a national park, they would need a parade permit, a series of wilderness camping permits (providing that they had reservations in advance), and liability insurance, and they would probably have to post a bond to ensure that they would do no ecological damage. Trails—new trails—are now known as "impact," just as any contemporary pictograph is considered vandalism.

The Ute Trail impacted the tundra with a yard-wide groove through the thin soil and several fire rings where the Indians camped. The wheel inventors came along next and showed the Indians how to make an impact that would be more resistant to weather and to vegetative reclamation. The first automobile road to go "up top" was laid out in 1911, and soon the engineers of speed and progress were happily dynamiting switchbacks up the ridges, slashing through the forests, and filling the valleys with crushed mountains.

When construction began on the Fall River side of the Divide, it was done by convicts. Warden Tom Tynan took his crews—called "Tom Tynan's boys"—into the national park, where their first job was to cut down trees and build themselves log cabins. When I was a boy, I could hike to the remains of those cabins, and today I ski and hike through that same clearing that the convicts cut. In today's Rocky Mountain National Park, such a camp would be unthinkable. Today's work crews live in cabins outside the park and are bussed to work each day. Trees are cut only if the proper impact statements have been filled out.

Convicts could not be used today, either. Human rights groups would see to that. Breaking rock, hauling materials by hand, shoveling gravel at ten thousand to nearly twelve thousand feet of elevation? Cruel and inhuman. At the time, apparently, it was not human rights but politics that put an end to the use of convict labor crews. Colorado penitentiary wardens, not too many years ago, were big political figures. So was the controversial superintendent of Rocky Mountain National Park. The state was paying for the road, which would become U.S. Highway 34 in the course of time, but park administrators insisted upon saying exactly where and how the road should be built. The question of who would get the contract, and from whom, and whether commercial transportation within the park would be freely competitive or monopolistic, almost kept the road from being built at all.

Fall River Road eventually opened in 1920. It linked the towns of Estes Park and Grand Lake, Colorado, and created new vehicular thrills for the tourists while it boosted both towns into the vacation business. Fights over control of the road continued, and in earnest. Enos Mills, who had been instrumental in establishing Rocky Mountain National Park, now found himself fighting against a park administration that wanted to issue a monopolistic license; under their plan, *one* transportation company would be allowed to run buses on Fall River Road. Enos Mills died in 1922, but the jurisdictional battle went on and on. When Colorado's political winds shifted, the new state officials finally gave up; in 1929, the state turned the governance of the road over to national park authorities.

The effect was immediate: the Rocky Mountain National Park superintendent's office announced plans to build a better route. "Better," in this case, meant more capacity for traffic. Today this highway is known as Trail Ridge Road, and it is an ecological scar of such costly proportions that today's national park officials admit that it should never have been built. Given our concern for environment nowadays, and the cost of building a highway under ecological impact rules, Trail Ridge would be a political impossibility.

∾

Our bus leaves the campground and begins the long uphill crawl toward the Continental Divide on Trail Ridge. Professor Tom Lyon, one of my two colleagues on the Wilderness Experience, is eager to get the students out onto the tundra, but we balk at using the usual tourist spots, those places where rangers have built redwood walkways and have erected metal signs that "interpret" the flora. This is a nature-writing class, and we are not here to read our lessons from government plaques.

Joe Gordon sports a baseball cap emblazoned with his administrative title: "El Jefe." He keeps leaning across the aisle of the bus to show me a dotted line on his souvenir map of the park. The old Ute Trail. When we get to it, he says, we'll stop and let the students out so that they can hike the trail. We will meet them further up the road at the visitor center. I keep trying to explain that while there *is* a trail, up above timberline it fades. In many places, there are only stone cairns indicating where the rangers think the original trail was. Tom and I vote down the idea of turning the students loose up here with only a sketchy map to follow and several miles of tundra to negotiate. Joe hired us because of what we know about mountains; and we know, from experience, that this tundra only *seems* benign, with its tiny flowers and cushion tufts of grass and outcrops of storm-softened granite. There are crevices in it; its distances are deceptive; exhaustion comes easily at two miles above sea level, and so does hypothermia. Tundra offers the inexperienced enthusiast a dozen ways to vanish, to die.

If El Jeffe wants to lose the students, he will have to do it elsewhere. I can't have all those breakfast-bloated cadavers rotting away on the watershed of my childhood river.

This is the rooftop of the North American continent, where no trees grow. The summer, which is only eight weeks long from snowmelt to snowfall, brings lumpy patches like faded bulges of velvet in between the hard-cornered granite rocks. They are miniature rock gardens, struggling reservations of extremely vulnerable vegetation. So, before letting the students out of the bus to run amok, I start exercising my professorial authority. First, I instruct them to stay on the rocks and off the vegetation wherever possible. We are going to hike up a small peak behind the visitor center, but there is no "official" trail and so we have to protect the tundra as we go. I warn them not to run, although I don't really need to bother: the air at twelve thousand feet seems devoid not only of all pollution, but of oxygen as well. Running a few steps makes the lungs burn. It is also air that is refrigerated: a sudden huge gulp of it chills the curve at the back of your mouth and even makes your teeth hurt.

In defiance of my professorial wisdom, or as a joke on me, nature has placed the tundra rocks much too far apart. It has been a wet and early spring, so the moss-pads and the islands of flowers have turned into a virtual carpet. It is impossible not to step on flowers. The students begin mocking my instructions as they spread out to go up the mountain. "Watch out there, Fred. You stepped on an itsy flower!" "Maybe we were supposed to bring rocks from the parking lot."

I find Tom and we finish the climb together, separating ourselves from the chattering clusters of students. He points in excitement at the number of flowers that are here and can name every one of them. A dozen species are in bloom simultaneously. We carefully step around flax, phlox, sky pilot, alpine daisy, miniature violets with heads smaller than shirt buttons, alpine clover and king's crown. King's crown displays shade after shade of lavender, the lavender giving way to brilliant whites and hypnotic blues, which blend with regal shades of purple and soft moss green. The whole plant would make a perfect cushion on which to display emeralds. It has thousands of perfect lilliputian blossoms in a patch no larger than a tea-saucer; tiny green leaves and flowers ranging from pink to deep purple transform it into a living nosegay. This particular specimen is probably a hundred years old, with a taproot reaching down six feet into the cold granite crack.

Lie down. Get yourself nose-close to the fuzzy short grass between these elfin bouquets of jewel-flowers, and you will see that there is also a whole world of animal life on the tundra. This half-moon depression in a spot of glacial sand is the track of a young elk who crossed over the divide early this morning. The dew was still on the soil, making it soft enough to take his imprint. Over here are some droppings of the little pika, and over there are places where the grass has been neatly nipped off at the base and carried away. So! The tundra rodent is busily harvesting his hay to stockpile against winter. Here you see his little crop of grass spread on a rock to dry; that white mark next to the pika's food is the rude splatter from a raven's digestive tract, dropped here as he stood clutching this granite outcrop, leaning streamlined with squinting eyes into the cold wind. He is a true raven, this black giant of the tundra—bigger than any mere crow, and a predator as well as a scavenger. Next to you there—that topless tunnel, that groove in the grass, is the architecture of the vole, a kind of mountain mouse. When the snowpack was heavy up here, the voles cut tunnels in the matted grass, with the snow as the roof. The tunnels led from the burrows to the foodstores. And then the snow melted, leaving these troughs where tunnels used to be. In this particular trough, we see a sharp set of little tracks, but not the tracks of a vole: a high country weasel (an ermine, before May came) has found the route and followed it with hungry enthusiasm.

You found the ladybug eggs on the underside of that flower leaf, did you? The ladybugs feed on gnats' eggs too small for you to see, even with a field lens, and on the microscopic larvae of minuscule ants. In turn, the pretty little horned lark who lives up here, that lovely bird with the lyrical morning song, feeds upon ladybugs. Bring your magnifier over here. Look at this dead horsefly. The body is scissored neatly in half, bisected, dead evidence of a horned lark snapping at a fly in midair. If you don't believe me, just watch the larks awhile as they devastate the horsefly population.

The body of our unfortunate insect—or this half of it, at least—lies amid mushrooms. Want to duplicate a mushroom this size? Take an eighth of an inch of orange spaghetti. Hollow one end of it and flare it out into a goblet shape, like a fairy thimble. Stick the other end in the ground. Now, add a hundred or more like it, and you will have a little mushroom jungle about the size of a quarter. These mushrooms are so small that a hundred of them cannot conceal half of a dead fly.

If you lie there long enough in the sun-warmed tundra, you will feel the granite mountain breathing and will hear its eternal heartbeat. You may not feel it in the sense of being able to call to a friend and say, "Come here! Listen to this mountain!" But if you remain there long enough, the beat of your own heart will match pace with the mountain's tempo, and your breathing will mimic the rising and falling of the tundra breeze. Stay until your body temperature is the temperature of the plants. Lie there; give yourself to the breathings, to the pulse, to the spirit of that place. You will begin to sense that our species did not rise from some steamy ooze; it did not crawl out of the sludgy glop of a long-since-fossilized swamp; the man-animal realized its essence on a tundra slope two miles above the sea. Up there, higher than the topmost trickle of my river, you can begin to feel that the beginning happened only yesterday, and could happen again today.

Following Where the River Begins • The Continental Divide

Earlier in the year, in the avalanche season when the mountains nonchalantly shrug off the crusty cornices of winter, you might put your body to the earth and hear and feel a rumbling like the beginning of distant thunder. Thomas Hornsby Ferril, Colorado's poet laureate, wrote that it is the sound of the mountains falling down, that grain by granule and block by cliff they are destined to crumble and float down the snowmelt rivers to become forever seashore on some far-off sandy coast. But I have listened to this sound of the mountains rousing themselves in spring, and I believe it means that they are reaching for the sky.

～

The students gather again at the parking lot, having taken their snapshots and bought their candy bars and souvenirs at the tourist center. Loaded once more, the bus faces away from the tundra serenity and starts backfiring its way down the western slope of the Rockies like an old grouch plagued with morning flatulence. Down we roll, back down past the lower limit of the treeless alpine zone, down through the ship-mast stands of subalpine firs and spruces, back down into the gloomy green montane zone of lodgepoles and ponderosas. We catch a glimpse of the infant Colorado River, like a trickle of poured mercury shining across open beaver meadows and melting again into deep forests. I watch from the bus window until I can't see the river anymore and make myself a silent promise to come back, later, alone, and walk clear up to the headwaters of the river, to see for myself a place I have heard of. Up at the very top of the headwaters is a region of oddly shaped ocherous rock formations marked on the map as the "Little Yellowstone."

The bus squeals and wheezes to a stop at the Rocky Mountain National Park Visitor Center. Riding along thinking about a solo trip into the Little Yellowstone, I have developed a sudden case of cartographic fever. This ailment, common to many who want to be anywhere but where they are, is marked by a fascination for maps. Sufferers like me can spend hours staring at little wavy lines and exotic place-names, endlessly interpreting each contour. When the sickness hits me, I hunch over a map for hours, tracing unknown rivers from headwaters to confluences.

I head straight for the visitor center bookstore to buy a "quad" map of the park. I also inventory the selection of guidebooks and texts on flora and geology. The students, meanwhile, head straight for the restrooms.

They glance disinterestedly at the displays on their way out of the building, buy cans of cold pop from the machine outside, and climb back aboard the bus to relax.

On the road again. Once we are past Grand Lake Village, the temperature begins to rise to uncomfortable levels. Soon we are beyond the deep ponderosa forests and out into sagebrush valleys bordered by rounded hills. From here on, the only tree zone we will see will be the "P-J" region—piñon and juniper.

El Jeffe tells Harold to pull off the road and stop. He pulls out another of his free maps, a torn relic from the days when service stations actually gave them away. He and Harold study a thin blue line that crosses a rip in one of the folds. Tom and I lean over and try to get a look at it. The blue line appears to be a dirt road offering us a shortcut. And in keeping with the announced plan of this trip, the road also follows the Colorado River. More or less. It could be too narrow for our bus in places. "*One* place would be enough," growls Harold. There could be bridges of questionable load capacity. How much does the bus weigh, anyway? "Too much," says Harold. The road could have steep grades in it, and we recall only too well how the old diesel engine had to strain to get the bus, the passengers, and the luggage up to the top of Trail Ridge Road. Shall we look for this cut-off and take it or not?

Go for it.

And so, near the village of Kremmling, Harold wheels the bus off the blacktop and onto a narrow dirt track that leads along the side of a treeless, sage-covered hill. Heavy with fuel and students and packs and supplies, the bus grumbles up and up and up the dirt road, shouldering itself between sagebrush thickets and slopes covered with Indian paintbrush. Near the top of the ascent, the road hangs on the side of a cliff. A couple of the guys lean out of their windows and reassure the rest of us that only the *outside* tires of the duals are hanging over the edge of the roadbed. "Saves the rubber," Harold says through clenched teeth.

A general sigh of relief breaks out when the road gets around the last corner of the precipice and the land opens out onto the Colorado River— broad, more silver than blue under the columbine sky, calm, quietly flowing. Inviting. The road leading down to it is wider and less steep; we all sit back, release our death grips on the armrests, and listen to the sound of the bus grinding along in second and third gear, heading for a place that Joe's road map calls "State Bridge," where we will intersect the wide and paved highway that goes to Glenwood Springs.

Following Where the River Begins • The Continental Divide

I like this river. I have invested thousands of hours in the pursuit of trout, standing in icy rivers throwing away tiny steel hooks expensively decorated with feathers and tinsel. I still know next to nothing about trout, but those hours have introduced me to the unique personalities of many and sundry rivers. The Snake River seems deep and ominous, not a comfortable river in which to wade. The Hoback is light and friendly, almost warm. The Poudre is "offish," as my mother would say—a disinterested river if ever there was one. With the Colorado, I expected to meet a belligerent river, a river that has been insulted with dams and wounded with irrigation gates and built upon and leveed into channels. A river with every reason to dislike the man-species.

Until this trip, the only part of the Colorado River I had known was the upper part, from the point where it meets Trail Ridge Road downstream to Grand Lake. Along that stretch, it is a clear mountain stream fed by alpine snowfields and numberless little springs that flow out of countless aspen groves. In its Rocky Mountain valleys, the Colorado surprises you with sudden trout pools. You step into what looks like a solid barrier of high spruce and fir trees, and suddenly in front of you is a flat and shining surface embossed with rings from the rising trout. At such moments of discovery, the Colorado seems like an actress dramatically sweeping open a dark green curtain to reveal an exotic stage setting. Step close to the edge and let me dazzle you, she seems to say to the fisherman, or stay where you are and my perfume will seduce your senses.

Down by Kremmling, on the way to State Bridge, it is different. This is a Colorado River that I have never fished. It bounces over hundreds of stretches of small rapids, reminding me of a girl laughing as she skips a slow-turning rope. A kid on an inner tube could play in this river, or could just sit on the bank and throw sticks into the current. Along the calmer portions, the water reflects a cornflower-blue sky in a mirror framed by silver hills. It is not the angry river that I was expecting. Where it parallels the paved highway to Glenwood Springs, it is confined by the cliff and the roadway, but it still has an open and personable quality to it. Further downstream, way down there in sandstone canyons where it boils and seethes and works itself up into an excessively assertive state, where its face becomes mud-brown from eating whole mesas, the Colorado River still seems to welcome its visitors to float along it in rafts, or stroll along its steep sides and look into all the various theaters of living geology and petrified botany. It would be a mistake to label this river benevolent or polite or even genteel. You might say that it gives an impression of being open-minded, and you will not often meet a river more candid than the Colorado.

PART THREE • THE CANYON OF WOODED GLENS

Two days and one hundred fifty miles from the scene of the Big Thompson flood, we find ourselves at the entrance to another narrow gorge through the Rockies. The Big Thompson Canyon is less than fifteen miles long and drains less than three hundred square miles of watershed. It is a small river, by river standards. In Estes Park, at the top of the canyon, the Thompson's flow is controlled by Olympus Dam.

Glenwood Canyon is less than fifteen miles long. In most places it is barely wide enough for the river, a railroad bed, and the highway. The river is not small. After leaving Rocky Mountain National Park, the Colorado River steadily acquires an increased water flow from countless small creeks along its way. More than a thousand square miles of watershed slope toward these creeks, with no significant dams to prevent it from funneling its floodwaters into the Colorado.

The dirt road we followed from Kremmling joins the main highway below State Bridge, and once again we are riding on asphalt. And once again we are approaching a narrow mountain canyon that was once the sole province of a powerful river. Below State Bridge, still in relatively open country, the Colorado picks up Antelope Creek, then Elk Creek and Sunnyside Creek, Big Alkali and Posey Creeks, Alamo Creek, and Poison Creek. It absorbs the waters of Red Dirt Creek and Willow Creek, Horse Creek, and the Sweetwater. At the town of Dotsero, the Colorado is joined by the Eagle River, which drains the snowmelt and summer rain from the mountains around Vail. Both rivers run unimpeded by major dams for dozens of miles, and at Dotsero they combine forces, pause at the edge of the plateau, and plunge together down Glenwood Canyon. The river picks up Spruce Creek, Cinnamon Creek, Devil's Hole Creek, the Deadman, and the Grizzly. At the town of Glenwood Springs it will be joined by combined contributions of the Crystal River and the Roaring Fork River, which bring water down from Aspen, Snowmass, and the Maroon Bells wilderness.

The Colorado River is now a serious consideration. She has that same open personality but seems candidly dangerous as well. One thinks of an attractive, charming western lady smiling at one across the sights of a cocked Winchester.

❦

Between the entrance to Glenwood Canyon and the town of Glenwood, it is not the river that seizes your attention. It is the canyon, and what has been done to it. It is a winding canyon that the river has cut through rugged granite, leaving wild rapids that throw spray onto delicate mosses. Undoubtedly there are also silvery trout and daring water-diving ouzels living in it. Once there were even glens of wildwood trees: cottonwood, river birch, aspen and conifers. But the canyon's primitive beauty does not capture your imagination. What captures your imagination and commands your attention is the highway that the humans have built. It, and not the river, now dominates the canyon. How did it happen that these two forces, the falling water and the engineered concrete shelf, came to use this narrow cleft in the mountains?

Centuries before there was any measurement of centuries—eon upon eon unmarked by the human animal—the melting snow and the falling rain drained across the immense plateau, cutting downward into the strata as the plateau continued to rise upward on the continental uplift. Icy waters from the high country and hot mineral waters from the canyon springs slowly wore away the rock. Frost came. Water in the cracks froze into ice, expanded, and cracked the granite. Tree roots went deep and then grew and swelled, keeping up the pressure, opening more faults for the icy waters of winter. The freezing and thawing and the heat of blistering summers worked away at the walls, and, whether millimeter by millimeter or a thousand tons at a crash, the granite mountain was undercut and fell into the rapids.

And the rapids pushed stone downstream for more endless centuries. It shoved barn-size boulders here and there and split them and erased them, ground them up and tumbled them. The canyon deepened into a gorge. Above the river's reach, the upper heights of the walls became calm and safe; the blowing dust of ages found places to rest among the cracks and tiny ledges; flower seeds and grass seeds found the pockets of dust; birds came and left tree seeds; and the lichen and mosses grew, and soon—oh, within a mere thousand years of time—the canyon was landscaped. A rock garden.

People with copper-colored skin came quietly in moccasins to walk along the river; the last of them were the Utes, who came this way each year to use the cleansing mineral waters at the mouth of the canyon. When they came to the narrows and saw the fractured granite ledges poised high above them, they walked quickly and with hushed voices. After the Utes came a race of louder people, people with blotchy pink skin, people wearing boots and riding on iron-shod horses, following the moccasin trail.

The first road they built, these booted humans, had to stay down low in the canyon and remained open only at the whim of the Colorado. After a time it seemed to fit into the scheme of the place. Then the first asphalt road came, and after a time its jet-black surface mellowed into a dingy dark gray, and even the glaring yellow highway signs became camouflaged by willow bushes, and it was a beautiful drive. "Let's take that beautiful drive up Glenwood Canyon," weekend travelers would say. "Let's open the windows and roll back the top and drive along listening to the water and listening to the echo of the canyon walls. Let's stop along the way and turn off the engine and listen."

Inevitably, these people who liked to drive themselves to different places found that they were more interested in getting to the places than in the process of getting there. Getting to Aspen. Getting to Vail. Getting to Glenwood or getting to Grand Junction. Getting on over to the Coast. Getting the heck out of the twisting canyons. And so they air-conditioned the cars and welded the car tops solid so that the passengers would not need to have the windows open or the top down. No longer would they hear the water or the echoes of the canyon. And since they were in a hurry to arrive somewhere, and since they could not smell the air or listen to the wild sounds, they decided to build a Better Highway. Four lanes, not two. Straighten the curves where you can. Bridge the river here, cut the cliff there, fill this bend, and you can make it four lanes wide. With four lanes, everyone can pass anyone, on their way to the place they told the passengers they would want to go. "You'll be wanting to go to Vail. We can get you there quicker than this. Four lanes!" "You'll be wanting to go to Utah, Nevada, California, and you want to hurry. Four lanes! Sixty-five miles per hour!"

For a few years, the canyon posed them a problem, because it was too high and too narrow to fit both the river and the four lanes (and of course there had to be wide shoulders, although it would be illegal to stop on them; the median strip had to be wide, so that travelers on the way down would not recognize the travelers on their way up). What to do? The engineers considered putting the river—the *Colorado River,* if you please!—into a tube under the roadbed, and then they could have the whole canyon floor to themselves. But the threat of flood—the cocked Winchester pointed downriver—frightened them. A huge and expensive series of dams would be needed to control the flow into the tube.

∾

Our bus is compelled to stop for a flagperson while some earthmovers rumble across the road in front of us. We have come to the point where the new construction is going on. I glare straight ahead at all the displaced earth and rock, at the monstrous yellow machines tearing up and down with loads of mountain on their backs, at a pitiful little pile of trees that has been bulldozed into a thin side canyon. I look at Tom, who shakes his head. I look back at the students. Some are sleeping. Some are reading. The rest are staring through the windows, their faces expressionless and bored. They would like to get moving again; they are looking forward to an afternoon swim in the hot springs pool at Glenwood.

I turn to face the windshield again and study the structure of the new highway, the engineers' obscene alternative to a river tube.

They knew as early as 1957 that there would be a four-lane road through this canyon. It was needed so that Interstate 70 could run without being interrupted by scenic bottlenecks. Moreover, it was a challenge and an opportunity for the people who build such things as highways and tunnels and bridges. And so it was inevitable. The Colorado State Legislature, the Highway Commission, and the Citizen's Advisory Committee talked about routes and talked about impact and talked about finances throughout the sixties; on February 20, 1976, A. J. Siccardi, division administrator for the Colorado Division of Federal Highway Administration, notified the chief engineer of the Colorado Division of Highways, E. N. Haase, that he could turn the earthmovers loose: Glenwood Canyon was to be the route.

One of the first things Haase's department did was to begin publication of a newsletter, *Canyon Echo,* in order to "keep everyone informed as to the events and progress." The newsletter promised that there would be no obnoxious visual impact made by the highway. It outlined schemes for including bike paths and boating facilities throughout the canyon; it showed photographs of the vegetation that existed along the old highway and explained how it would all be restored; it reassured "everyone" that, while "some rock cutting of cliff faces will be required," the rock cuts would be "as natural looking as possible."

In a 1976 issue of *Canyon Echo* there is a cross-sectional drawing showing where the supports for the elevated highway would be placed. The canyon, in this picture, is U-shaped, with the river at the bottom; T-shaped figures represent the supports. Two are in the river, one on the left and one on the right. These are crossed out: not feasible. Another T is high up on the south wall of the canyon, which is the steepest wall. It is crossed out: too expensive. On the other side, where the slope is somewhat milder, there is a T near the river, called the "lowline" support, and one further up the hill, called the "highline." Each has two lanes. Each elevates the highway far above the river and the treetops.

That is the solution I was looking at through the bus window. How do you install four wide lanes of fast traffic in an earth-crevice barely wide enough to hold its own river? To begin with, you raise the first two lanes on T-shaped supports high above the river, far from the canyon bottom, very far from the willow glens and the shiny bright pebbles of the stream, so high that you cannot see the water from the roadbed. Now stack the opposite two lanes on top, like the multilevel elevated highways in the canyons of big cities. But do not make it high enough for travelers to see up or out of Glenwood Canyon; just set it high enough to get the cars quickly to the places where the people want to be.

And now when you need to go somewhere on Interstate 70, you will be able to stay behind your tinted glass with your air conditioner (for heaven knows *what* condition the real canyon air might be in!), put your Sarcophagus GTL into "drive," and drive safely to . . . where? "Safely" is the key concept, with four lanes. Before there were four lanes, Glenwood Canyon saw more accidents than most other two-lane roads. Between 1970 and 1976, there were two hundred and forty-five accidents, with fifteen deaths. These accidents were the fault of the canyon.

Fifty-five accidents were caused by rocks that had fallen onto the highway. The twisting of the canyon prevented drivers from looking far ahead, and so a dozen accidents were caused by "improper passing." In thirteen accidents, the driver was apparently asleep (but not while passing); in sixteen other accidents, the driver was intoxicated; in thirty-five, the driver was speeding. Eighteen were rear-end collisions. Twenty-nine were sideswipes. Nobody knows what caused the rest.

Could the people be protected from Glenwood Canyon's many dangers? State Patrol Chief Wayne Keith estimated that to do so would mean increasing the patrol in the canyon from four officers to fourteen. This, he said, would reduce accidents and deaths to an "acceptable" level.

But it would cost an "unrealistic" $250,000 per year. Therefore, the legislature allocated money to rebuild the road and avoid this unrealistic expense. The 1978 allotment was one million dollars. The 1979 allotment was eleven million. Twenty-five million in 1980, nineteen million in 1981, and twenty-four million in 1982.

The canyon will no longer be responsible for accidents, with the new highway. Rocks will not fall into the path of cars. Animals will not be seen on the road. Cars will not run into cars. People in cars will not offend people in other cars. Anyone who is out of his car will be questioned by the Highway Patrol, whose job it is to see that you are not molested on your way to . . . where was it?

The traffic will move. It will move at a minimum of forty miles per hour, and a maximum of sixty-five, unless the government moves the limit back to fifty-five. I am told that the new, straight, high, stacked four-lane highway will enable the average person to get to Glenwood Springs in eight minutes less than on the "old" highway. However, with a higher average speed, it is more likely that each accident will cost a human life. More patrol officers will be needed, but at an acceptable cost. The life of the canyon, everything that goes into making it a community of living things, will also suffer a predictable cost; it cannot be computed on the available software.

What is *not* predictable is what the Colorado River will do if some hundred-year storm floods its far-reaching watershed. The new two-layered highway has done nothing to widen the canyon, or to control the river. The T-shaped supports *are* impressive monoliths, anchored in bedrock, and are said to be flood-proof. However, one remembers seeing television footage of collapsed two-level highways in California—highways that were earthquake-proof. Even if one does not remember pictures of collapsed highways, there is still a feeling of relief when the bus leaves the canyon and the shadows behind, when the bright late afternoon sun suddenly fills the windshield.

Tonight we will sleep in a Glenwood Springs hotel. Tomorrow night we will sleep at Arches, in Major Powell country, Abbey country.

PART FOUR • WINDMILLS AND NO WIND

Enos Mills was the pioneer advocate of Rocky Mountain National Park; John Muir was the patron saint of Yosemite; Arches is Abbeyland. Edward Abbey rangered here, back in the dirt road and low-traffic days; in 1968 he published a book about it, called *Desert Solitaire*. It is a truthful book, an on-the-spot book, and a book that comes from Abbey's intimate association with the landscape. His farewell thought, at the end of his season with the Department of the Interior, is part of a long, last look at the arches, the plants, and the sand canyons. "How difficult to imagine this place without a human presence; how necessary."

It was after I had taught *Desert Solitaire* several times that I learned that Abbey claimed to have written it in a bar in Hoboken. All the imagery, the atmosphere of desert and mountain, the immediacy of his experiences had been, in Wordsworth's phrase, "recollected in tranquility." This was difficult—if not impossible—to believe.

I have an irony to share with you: I once wanted to understand just why Willa Cather wrote about the Southwest, wanted to understand what she found there; therefore, I spent weeks looking for places she visited in New Mexico. But not once did I consider the most obvious fact about her southwest fiction: she didn't *write* it there. By the same token, I always wondered why Abbey had written *Desert Solitaire* in Hoboken rather than at Arches. Without looking for an answer, I found it. *Nobody* could write in a place like Arches.

Trying to write my journal here, I have a visible fog of no-see-um gnats swirling in my face. I take each breath through clenched teeth, trying not to inhale a swarm of them, and my scalp crawls at the thought that the little black demons are searching for blood among my hair roots. Back in Moab, a druggist sold me a special potion, a local formula guaranteed to keep them off. It smells like a weasel's armpit. It keeps the gnats from landing on my skin, all right, but it only attracts thousands more of them who hover an inch away from my face, trying to see what kind of creature would give off such a putrid odor. My sweat mixes with the insect goop and runs down my forehead, detours around my nose, runs a line of bitter vomit-acid taste across my lip, and drips onto the pages of my journal. Oddly, I don't care. When the pencil skids on a splotch of greasy sweat, I just write the next word anyway; in a minute I will even forget the word that should have been where the blotch is.

My mind is in slow gear. It is after 6:00 P.M. now; the air temperature is 104 degrees.

No wonder that Abbey played his games of *Solitaire* in that saloon in Hoboken, far from the sand fleas and stir-fried air. And even without the heat and the sweat and the slowing down of the brain, there are still the synapse-numbing distractions of Arches itself. Take, for instance, what I can see even in the limited vista that this campground offers. Better yet, join me. You'll have to excuse the smell. I've chosen this solar-heated redstone boulder to be my seat and my desk; tonight it will be my dining table and, with luck, my bar. Sit here. Close your eyes and imagine nothing but the color blue. Make it really deep blue, translucent plastic blue. Desert sky. Unrelieved, monotonous, bottomless blue arching overhead for—what?—a hundred miles in any direction you can look? Even downward. Stare at that blue void until it starts to turn black (it will, because you will begin to black out from staring at it), then look down at your feet in the sand and the sand and everything will still be blue. The heat rises in visible blue waves, at a hundred degrees of hot.

We can see some ranges of blue-gray mountains way off in the shimmering distance. They seem to have white tops. The map says that these are the La Sal Mountains, more than twelve thousand feet in elevation. Easily high enough for those white tops to be snowfields. But that must be a lie. Those snowy-looking summits must be mirages; today, the entire world is a hundred degrees. How could there be snow when there is such heat? My mind is convinced that the entire earth has turned into an oven; there cannot be a place that is not burning up. Snow cannot exist. Snow is just a dim, primitive memory.

The view from my stone desk includes mesas and monoliths of Navajo sandstone, piled up and blasted apart and cracked and wind-scoured into mesmerizing futuristic landscapes. Over there, about a half-canteen of water away from me, the shimmering pink sandstone formations are shaped like four mixing bowls overturned side by side on the land, touching each other; they stand four stories high. I would not want to see them in full moonlight: they might be giants from the furnace of hell, hiding their faces away from daylight in the earth, waiting for the night to come. Closer to me is a massive red sombrero made of stone, lying on the land. Not too much further away, I can see a weird collection of monoliths, resembling all shapes of mushrooms—tall ones, stubby ones, crooked ones. All stone, all several buildings high! Other monumental monoliths have odd caps, like petrified foreskins looking wrinkled and impotent. A sudden fantasy: I could be my own Dr. Frankenstein and assemble a living rock Colossus from the scattered bits of sculpture out there. Shelley's "Ozymandias" whizzes suddenly into my mind, unbidden, unexpected. "I met a traveler from an antique land," I begin to recite, and the gnats swarm away, startled. This human not only stinks, but he makes offensive noises as well.

Following Where the River Begins • Windmills and No Wind

There are feminine shapes in the sandstone, too. You do not notice them at first, but they clearly dominate the landscape. For each of the thrusting, assertive masculine formations there is the quiet, soft background of beckoning shadows. Everywhere, if you look for them, you will see elongated mounds that suggest the shape of a resting thigh; they lie there, hot and glowing in the evening air. The low light of late afternoon throws shadows across secret crevices. Shadows also accentuate breast-shaped formations, some as large as a mesa, some small enough to cup in my hand. Here and there you see light-colored sandstone that lies flat, swept clean of sand, and you again see the feminine form in the smoothness of it. There is one such shape below me; it looks like golden skin against the red sand and has a rise and fall like a woman's belly, even down to the gentle little indentation that looks like a navel. Then the light fails, and the shadows blur away. It is evening again.

From up here in the rocks, my mountain tent looks too small to hold as many memories as it does. It looks like a small shard of late afternoon sky, left behind by the retreating day heat. It seems to shimmer, like a mirage of a blue pond. Actually, it is too hot to have nylon walls, so I just put up the fly. It is pitched tight and staked out taut to catch the shade and let the breeze slip under the edges. Tonight in the desert dark those winds will be like warm breath, like dry breathing coming through my shade-shelter, and I will be sleeping on top of the sleeping bag, using it to insulate my body from the kiln-top sand. In the coolest part of the night I will wake, and be lonely again.

My tent site is in the stingy shade of a pitchy piñon pine, which at human height is the tallest piece of vegetation around here. The other midget trees are juniper, which give off a clean smell of gin and pine in the heat waves. Salt brush, a delicate light green like a junior prom taffeta, huddles in the depressions between sand drifts, sharing the meager windbreak with the fierce little cholla and the militant sharp Spanish bayonet—yucca. Sagebrush here seems aromatic and gentle; the bushes of mountain mahogany have a kind of somber dignity to them. The juniper are in season, heavy with those tiny bluish cones that look like berries or seeds. Some of the trees are so loaded with cone-berries that they look blue instead of green.

~

Each day at Arches brings a brief period of time when, perhaps, a person could concentrate on some writing. Most of the day is too sun-hot to think, but an hour after sunset, just before it gets dark enough to sleep, there comes a time of relief. You seem to be able to let your breath out for the first time that day. And, at least if you are like the people in our group, this time of day somehow makes you want to be alone. No Frisbee or Hacky Sack games, no gossip groups.

The students have scattered. Like me, they have gone to their individual rocks. The heat and the still air seem to have an antisocial effect. They have crept out of the shady spots where they were loafing, and they have moved up onto the rocks. Some are just sitting or lying there, and they resemble a colony of lizards come out to watch the last light of day die. A half-dozen other students are sitting on individual sandstone formations, dutifully doodling in their journals.

One particular rock at a distance from any of the lizards or doodlers has a thin Buddha sitting cross-legged on it, meditating in the classic position. Must be Tom. He's from Utah and a veteran desert-trekker. Tom has a strange double effect on me: on the one hand, he is one of those people who makes me want to hike and explore places; but he also has an addictive, quieting effect on my mind. His is a spirit in which there is an omnipresent enthusiasm running in a slow current of gentle intensity. One of those genuinely gentle men you sometimes find in the world. One evening at Arches, a couple of the students asked Tom to teach them to meditate. Since they had an hour to spare between eating and sleeping, they thought it would be amusing to practice some transcendent wisdom. Not that they needed it. Tom coached them into a simple beginning position, and they sat there dutifully staring off into space. Later, some wrote in their journals that it had been a truly religious experience, floating off into the ether of the pure mind and leaving the dross of the body behind. It's amazing what young people can accomplish—or imagine that they accomplish.

Joe "El Jeffe" Gordon, by comparison, exhausts students. I can see him now, walking toward the bus down there. Joe strikes me as a man who is always going somewhere, always on the move to do something, arrange something, check on something. I have shared his living room with him and have seen him sit there in front of the television, a beer in his hand and the paper on his lap, and I still had the distinct feeling that he was about to get up and do something. Hiking with him is a surprise, too. He starts off at a quick pace, like an inexperienced walker who begins at a gallop and soon is shuffling along, all tired out. With Joe, the gallop just goes on mile after mile, all day long.

He's a physical man in fine shape. On a trip such as this, his treatment of the students is linked to the physical aspect in many ways. Tom will sit and listen to them. Joe will listen, but he is more likely to make them walk with him while he does. He goes around while they set up camp, throwing out bits of insight regarding the reading assignment or facts about the local flora and geology, questioning them while they work. Tom accepts student chatter with quiet encouragement; Joe ridicules stupid remarks, challenges almost every generalization, insists on solid logic and genuine insights from them.

Intellectually, Joe is like Thomas Huxley's metaphoric steam engine, with all parts in order and able to turn to any kind of work. One moment, with dogged, ponderous power he is working away at some big decision. A moment later, with his mental gears set on "fast whiz," he indulges in verbal fencing matches. Then, back in second or third gear, Joe sorts and turns the day's routine matters into neat piles. I love to watch him pick his way through an hour-and-a-half lecture—he works basically without notes—and I *really* love trying to sidetrack him with irrelevant ideas. When I deliberately introduce a tangential topic, Joe will take out around me, set up a few open switches or roadblocks just down the line, and then throttle back to where he was going to go in the first place.

～

As for our students, they are—well, young. Awfully, awfully young. Their youth is probably why I dislike having them call me "Jim" rather than "Professor." It's a campus custom, but I could do without it. I dislike the way they talk about all the experiences they have had, all around the world . . . not because I'm jealous, but because I resent how very little they have made of those experiences. Most of them are intellectually soft, with minds like a soft avocado. Their conversation is lackluster, limpid, uninteresting; they have been philosophically spoon-fed and emotionally pampered all their lives. I want them to get overenthusiastic, or despondent, or irate, or *anything*. To call their usual state of mind "apathy" would be to dignify it.

There are two students on this trip—just two—who have some idea of what emotion means. They have both been through emotional trauma recently. I don't know if I like them because they confided in me, or because they are different from the others in at least one regard, or because I'm just anxious to justify my role as teacher. They came to me in regard to the journal assignment. One had witnessed the automobile death of her best friend and couldn't be alone with her journal without flooding its pages with grief. The other had surprised his fiancée with another guy in bed. He couldn't think straight enough to write *anything* in a journal. He couldn't stand to be alone with himself that long.

As I said, I don't know exactly why these particular students got a response out of me. Like me, I suppose, they have trouble reconciling their situation with their needs, their responsibilities with their impulse to run and hide. Before I knew about these two cases, the class was discussing the use of simile and metaphor. Several had used the equivalent of "I was thrilled" or "I was happy" in their essays, and I challenged them to *show* it, to make the reader feel thrilled or happy. "Grief," I said. "What is grief *like?*" We came up with a simile. "Heartbreak sounds like the ripping of blood-soaked gauze." These two students, I was later to learn, did not find the simile exaggerated.

The four students who irritate me most—if one can actually be irritated by trivial people—are all slightly overweight, slightly overdressed, slightly vain, and slightly too cool to be with the rest of the group. They hang out together to share cigarettes. They talk in phony voices and without looking at each other. The conversations are ritualistic round-robins of high school stories. One girl looks at the tip of her cigarette, or up at the sky—not at the listeners who are not looking at her—and tells how she, like, really like totally *trashed* her parents' new car; then the next one interrupts with her tale of how—wow—these totally awesome dudes had like even a cooler car than *that,* and took her and her really close, y'know, girlfriend on a totally bogus road trip. Wow, she used her parents' plastic and they like got a bill for two *thousand* dollars from like Visa? and were *totally* bent. Totally bogus event. Bogus, in their dialect, means "fine."

Ego filling is fine with me. Who doesn't do it? But I hate the way these kids will switch on their feigned sincerity all the time. With me, for instance, they switch it on to try to find out "what I want" on the essays that are due. They lean toward me and look at me earnestly and let me know how totally great it is to get alone and like experience the wilderness and how much, much, much they want to learn about themselves and about nature. Their writing is junk generalization and cliché, but they try to convince me that they have had all sorts of religio-ecological revelations on our encounter with nature.

By the time this class ends and our field trip is over, each one will have had several mandatory conferences with me. And each one will feel he or she deserves a good grade even without finishing the required essay. They have been brought up to believe that confession means automatic absolution, instant cleaning of the slate. Everything in their world can be "made up." When one of these misses a test or doesn't get an essay assignment written, the question is invariably the same: "How do I make it up?" If they are absent, the question is the same: "How do I make it up?" The question is never *"Can* I make it up?" and often the answer is no. "No, I will not give you a make-up test. No, I will not just forget about the paper assignment when I figure out the grades. No, I will not repeat the entire hour's lecture for your benefit." Life, they will find, can't be "made up" when it is missed.

And so I sit in the twilight, seeing Freudian shapes in the sandstone. In just three days, I have already made a bad job of it. Two students need to be forced to look at our surroundings, need to be coerced and badgered into some therapeutic writing. But I am too aware of their problems to do it. Too sympathetic. With the others, apathy is the problem. Or antipathy. Sometimes this job has more challenge than it really needs.

I take a last look at Abbey's country before turning in. I had an idea for a T-shirt design once: it would have Abbey on the front of it, caricatured with armor and a lance and looking like Don Quixote. "So many windmills," it would say, "and so little time." A few months before his death, I received a copy of *The Fool's Progress;* inside, Abbey had written, "To Jim. You're right: there are a lot of windmills."

Maybe each lizard-student of mine is a windmill. And not a breath of wind to be had. Any sign of movement would be welcome, here in the hot night country.

PART FIVE • SCOPING THE ARK

The two-mile walk to Landscape Arch is best taken at sunset. At that time of day, the shadows will be growing long and the heat will still be intense. The sun will be directly in your face as you go up, and the trail will be dark and hard to follow as you come down again. But it is the best time to go, because it is in those closing hours of daylight that the desert can make an acute observer out of you.

You are going to feel overheated and thirsty even before leaving the trailhead and starting up the trail. You will feel the skin of your face shrinking and roasting under that horizontal solar broiler; the sensation makes me think of those barbecued chicken carcasses that turn on spits in supermarket delicatessens. This feeling that your face is turning into a crispy entrée is good: it makes you attentive to the trail. It is the desert's way of getting your attention. Before venturing into the narrow sandstone alley at the very beginning of the trail, you will probably take careful notice of where you are and how far you will be going and in what direction you intend to go. Back at home, when I walk out of my house, I habitually pat my pocket to see if I have my keys. At Arches, I shake my canteen to see that it's full and take a bearing on my surroundings.

The narrow alley I mentioned is a redstone passageway, easy to confuse with a hundred others. The floor is sand, and the walls curve gracefully inward, overhead. There are a few clusters of sage and cactus and juniper, huddled close to the base of the wall.

When you walk in the city, you see so many things in motion that you tend to see none of them. In the desert, there are very few things that move, and so you tend to notice them. It might be a little windspout whirling over the horizon, or a lizard darting up a nearby rock. Along the Landscape Arch trail, you will notice more birds, not because there are more of them here than elsewhere, but because they are more constantly in motion than anything else in the area. Many of them are daytime foragers, but at sunset the desert launches her best fliers. The nighthawk, a little swept-wing gray falcon with white wing strips, makes its "keeeeaaaahee" cry each time it goes into a steep banking maneuver and accelerates after an airborne bug. The wings are thin, sharply bent backward in the middle of the leading edge, sharply pointed at the tip, built for effortless sustained soaring and for breathless downward dives.

The other flier is a true night fighter, getting an early start before the dim dusk turns to black. When you spot the first one of these, you will think that it is a shadow in your eye. You might see it as an optical illusion, a tiny bug flying close to your face. It sometimes makes a small, faraway noise, and it is shaped almost like a housefly or a moth. Then you see more of them. Here they come, flying down the alleyway in bandit formation, pulling up as they reach you, going into a tight fast turn. Each one turns as if it had a wingtip thumbtacked to the sky. Then they dip into a free fall and then easily rise again to the top of the alley wall. Wings like sails, like sport parachutes, only chunky and leathery. The nighthawk may justifiably exult in its gracefulness, in the sheer aesthetics of narrow-wing flight, but the bat seems more interested in being quick and effective than in being beautiful. It is quiet Death in motion—and flies as if it knows it.

The sun setting behind the slickrock shapes will burn images into your awareness. At your feet, long shadows are flat carbon copies of the stone forms that loom ahead. The horizon beyond the rocks looks like goblin silhouettes cut out of hot thin tin, backlit by an eerie orange sky. The extraterrestrial light of evening is blue-orange and orange-black. Dead juniper trees along the trail hold their desiccated branches away from their twisted trunks as if in agony. You hurry around a corner to get away from them. You come up a slight hill between sand dune and rock, and the sun hits you full in the face; this time it is as bright as a carbon-arc spotlight. It seems as if the sun has exploded at the instant of sunset.

And now you are wading in knee-deep shadows and you begin to wonder whether the sidewinders and rattlers are coming out to lie on the warm trail; you wonder if the scorpions and the tarantulas saw the sunset from their shaded dens and are now on their way out for the evening hunting. After all, the bats are already out. Do you watch the sky for bats, or the trail for the slower-moving hunters? Actually, you look for a familiar formation so that you can get your bearings, but suddenly a sunset trick of the shadows makes that formation look unfamiliar. Your mind—the rational one—knows that it is the same stone monolith as before, but some other mind of yours can simultaneously believe just the opposite.

You will also distrust your senses when you come over that final rise in the sand and see Landscape Arch there before you. You must have strayed onto the trail to another arch: this soaring sliver of curved stone, this pink thin rainbow arched over the debris-choked canyon, is probably called Delicate Arch, or Fragile Arch. But it is Landscape Arch, which is a way of saying that names matter very little.

Almost three hundred feet from base to base, this is the longest known natural arch in the world. To imagine how thin it is, and how graceful, start with a picture of two tall Egyptian obelisks, standing three hundred feet apart. No, first you have to imagine three hundred feet. Think of the largest football stadium you can remember. The football field there is three hundred feet long, so this arch would reach from one set of end bleachers into the other end. It would soar above the grandstand.

Now imagine those Egyptian obelisks again. Imagine what they would look like if they began to melt in the desert sun, curving toward each other until the thin tips meet. The bases have slumped but are still square at the bottom. Stand here and imagine yourself climbing up there on the arch—it is a hundred feet up there—and the thought will make you dizzy.

I find myself almost hypnotized as I stand at the base of one of the legs. I am inside the arch, leaning back against the warm flat face of the arch rock, and the rock stretches upward from my heels, along my spine, and curves over my head; it continues the same curve, up and over and up and over and on and on to the center of the span, and it grows narrower and narrower as it curves, and narrower and narrower still, still flat-surfaced and still soaring, and becomes an optical illusion.

The problem I have is that I cannot make my mind register the fact that the rock tapers toward the span's center. It is something like looking down a long railroad track and not being able to believe that the two parallel tracks do not converge out there in the distance. This illusion is just the reverse of that: the long span of rock does *not* taper, says my head, and therefore the slim center of this reach of stone is the *same* dimension as this block against which I am leaning, and *therefore* the structure is so long that the base of the other leg must be perched on the nether edge of eternity.

Call it vertigo, or tell me it is only a phenomenon of failing light. The mind can do odd things with perspective. Falling down through the thin sky in your disabled airplane, watching your altimeter unwind at a rate of fifty-eight feet per second, it is possible to have the sensation that the earth is moving away from you at the same speed and you will never reach it. I was in a mystery house once, where the rooms look plumb and square and everything looks level—until the guide drops a ball and it rolls quickly *up* the floor and out the door—or until you turn the tap at a sink and the water runs out sideways. I have seen it, can explain it, and know it is an illusion. Maybe my mind sees an extra dimension sometimes, or is short on one dimension. Whichever the case, I am content to let others see that Landscape Arch actually tapers toward the center, if they will be content to let me see it touching down at the margin of eternity. What *we* see doesn't matter: the stone knows where it touches earth and where it touches sky, and what its name is.

I said that "Landscape Arch" seems like a pretty tame name for this ossified red rainbow. Over a year after being there, I dug into my old copy of Skeat's *Etymological Dictionary* and found out that the name is less of a misnomer than I thought. "Arch," according to Skeat, has Latin origins that have nothing to do with curving bridgelike structures. In Latin the word *arcum* means "bow-shaped" and gives us the word *arc*, which people confused with *arca*. The latter refers to a box or coffer, an "ark" used to carry things in, like the ark of the covenant. "Landscape" comes from two Middle Dutch words. *Land* means "region" or "area": the *-scap* part means "condition" and is a collective suffix. So, if we put the words together, we have an ark that safeguards the condition of the collective region. And that's true.

Like everything else in the desert slickrock country, Landscape Arch has ancient origins and is in the ages-slow process of metamorphosing into other forms. All the material that has fallen away from it has become sand again and may become sandstone again, given time. Like everything else out here, the aging effect is very visible in the rock because there is no overgrowth to hide it. Like everything else in the arch and canyon region, it has taken a form that seems to have no natural function. If it is a bridge, it is a bridge over the wind. Will any humans be there to hear it when the arch's end comes, or will the arch be alone again in the thunder of its final collapse?

It amuses me to hear some arch-watchers speak about "falling" and "collapsing" and to read the ranger-written signs that use the words "erosion" and "decay." This is the short view of things. The arches are not eroding—merely re-forming. There are more arches waiting to take the place of the fallen ones, unborn and buried in the sandstone mesas. The sand of former arches is going down the Colorado River right now, into the sea to be ocean-pressed into stone again and thence once more into arches. The rain washes tiny grains away from cracked blocks that mark the place where an arch used to span a gorge; those grains are the arch being taken to the seabed to become arches again on some other side of eternity. I suppose it reassures us, we who have such short spans ourselves, to smugly tell one another that even the rocks are in a state of "decay."

Time to go. Some of the students are disappointed because this arch was so close to the camp, and because we saw only one arch on this hike. Although none of us has sufficient philosophy to comprehend the miracle of this single arc of stone, they are ready to go "look" at another and another. They want to go "arch-bagging," the way some mountain hikers like to "bag peaks" at the rate of two or three a day, or the way tourists like to take in a half-dozen European cathedrals in a week's time.

Perspective again, I guess. They want quantity of experience; I want quality. Those two special students, the ones with the special emotional states of mind, have become blended into the group. From where I am, I see several bunches of students and can't distinguish anything but the colors of their clothes. I can tell myself that they are all individuals with individual needs and inclinations and thoughts and souls, but from here I can't see them. My interest in them fades; from here, they are finite and short-term features on an ageless landscape. Whatever I teach them, I realize, inevitably will turn to dust and will be gone.

As we make the walk back from Landscape Arch, the sunset-fire has burned down to embers and is safely banked behind a devil's backbone of phantasmagoric stone silhouettes. The bats and nighthawks are still veering and diving up there in the darker sky, and a little breeze from a side canyon carries the scent of piñon pines . . . the fragrance is coming from soft beads of yellow resin standing like droplets of perspiration on the heat-cracked bark.

~

Now, as I lie on top of my sleeping bag, I mentally review the trip, trying to figure out why I feel so detached from it. Thanks to all the years I spent studying the British poets, some lines from Wordsworth come to me and seem appropriate:

> And, more than all, a strangeness in the mind,
> A feeling that I was not for that hour,
> Nor for that place.
> —*The Prelude* 3.79–81

And that, in turn, leads to thoughts of Byron's frequent feelings of alienation from "the race of men," and I suddenly have the answer. The river. Byron habitually associated his blackest moods with deserts or mountains, seeing in the arid climates a metaphor for desiccated inspiration. Conversely, he wrote his most joyful verses when he was beside a river or sailing a lake or ocean. The ocean storms were "delightful terror" to him, and "clear, placid" Lake Léman tempted him to "forsake Earth's troubled waters for a purer spring."

So far on this trip we have not touched water. We have driven beside the Big Thompson River and followed the Colorado River. Some of the students even swam in the filtered and concrete-confined hot springs of Glenwood. But we have never got down next to the rivers to feel them. All my life I have been fascinated by the rushing rivers; as a boy, I used to hold sticks in Fall River just to feel the power of the current. Later, as a fly fisherman, I came to know the way a fast stream can swirl around the legs and the sensation of a trout on the line fighting both the water and the elasticity of my rod.

Perhaps I need to see rivers once in a while just because I am a native of the West, where the annual rainfall is fourteen inches or less and where water takes on special value. Perhaps rivers have become expressions of my life and determine what my mood will be. I finally drift into sleep, wondering if my dry and barren mood will become a thing of the past once we get back to where the Colorado River flows.

 ~

See if this sounds familiar. You go to bed and lie there wide awake for two hours. Then you get groggy but keep twisting this way and that in an effort to get comfortable. Finally, the deep and quiet sleep comes. And the next thing you know, somebody is shaking you by the shoulder to wake you up.

I come out of a dream and expect to see early sunshine with the slickrock and mesas starting to glow against a blue sky. Instead, I am staring into a black sky punctuated with stars. Some of them are blotted out by a skinny silhouette leaning over me. Tom has struck again. Flashlight. Wristwatch. *Four A.M.* He walks away from me just as I begin a vociferous speculation as to the legitimacy of his birth and goes on through camp, waking everybody. Before any of us is fully awake, we are in the bus and headed for Delicate Arch trailhead. He wants to get there before sunrise.

And get there we do. Long before the sun streaks the tips of the highest mesa, we are on the trail. I am carrying an orange that I have managed to purloin from the food box in lieu of breakfast, a canteen for the thirst to come, and a notebook and camera. It makes me feel overburdened as I scurry along alternately trotting and striding in my attempt to keep up with the lean prophet in sandals. I never could walk fast or jog early in the morning; I think I have one of those bodies that can't exert itself without an hour or two of warm-up.

Not that I don't enjoy a morning stroll; it's a pleasant experience to gradually awaken during a walk. I like the sensation of suddenly realizing where I am. Can't remember much about getting there, but there I am. Once in a while it does me good to discover that I don't really need an elaborate breakfast, and I don't really need to wash my face and brush my teeth and attend to all the other little silly duties before being able to "start" the day. I can just get up and do the main event and skip the ritual of preliminaries.

I usually spend an hour getting myself ready for the day—while the day has already started without me.

Tom talks excitedly as we climb up the sandy trail and over the stretches of slickrock. I try to make it a conversation, but he is setting a pace that pretty well prevents it from being a two-way talk. We stay ahead of the students, and when we finally pause to let them catch up we see that they have split up into two different groups, going along two different routes over the rock. Tom goes after the nearest bunch and herds them off to rejoin the other group. I volunteer to stay behind and take pictures and round up the strays. And maybe catch up on some breathing.

Have you ever hiked on slickrock, long-sloping slickrock? Wonderful vast expanses of slickrock? Most of it isn't slick at all; it's more the texture of fine red sandpaper laid out on easy contours. Distance on it is awfully deceptive: I look up a long slickrock slope at a line of cairns marking the trail and think, "What a waste of labor to put those markers so close together." But, in actuality, the distance from one pile of stones to the next is long and tiring. In another place, I find the opposite phenomenon. Seen from across a deep draw, a redrock formation looks high and inaccessible. But it takes me only a few minutes to climb up to it, and the walk is as easy as a staircase. Below this rock formation there is a natural amphitheater that looks as if an ice cream scoop has been used to gouge a cave into the rock. I call to it, just to hear the echo of my own voice. "Heyah eeeh!" Nothing comes back, at least not immediately. Then a faint "yah eeeh" comes from somewhere far away. What I had thought to be a modest-sized scoop in the rock is actually an immense cavity, more than a half-mile from me.

Slickrock. Slickrock is walking upslope and downslope, jumping down small ledges, putting hands to the warm stone to boost up over the ledge's edges, letting go and running like a kid down smooth stretches, marveling at a single bonsai juniper rooted in a rain-hollow, walking sideslope until the ankles begin to burn, circling all the way around gargantuan redstone shapes, shapes like marshmallows, like bread loaves, boot heels, sombreros, half-buried baked potatoes, fallen frankfurters. Slickrock makes you realize something very profound: an orange is not enough breakfast.

Up a slope you walk, loafing along the inclined level broadness of it, and suddenly you are above a whole maze of minor canyons, looking down into pure erosion. You make up names to fit the sizes and the shapes of these places, and each of the places seems awfully inviting to you—as if it has something unique and special to offer that none of the other little canyons has. What do you call them? Slots, valleys, slits; canyons, arroyos, fissures, crevices (one looks like a crevasse, sitting between two plump mounds that are like melted red ice); holes, amphitheaters, breaks; depressions, dips, washtubs, channels, alleyways, avenues . . . any name you can imagine, you can find slickrock to fit.

On the high places, the sandstone formations look as if they have been made with a giant's Jell-O mold.

It is exhilarating to run across the slickrock in the cool morning air. The feeling reminds me of when I was a kid and got new tennis shoes and could run like the wind. The mood changes quickly, however, when I get into the silty sand down in the bottom of the draws. I slog through the fine sand powder, and I get tired of it. Quickly. Little twinges of fatigue hit those muscles at the back of my legs, and I become aware that sweat is soaking my shirt. My mood is in tune with the terrain, which means that it is oscillating between a sort of deep elation and boyish buoyancy. The elation comes from the running and the easy walking and letting the quiet early morning desert act on my soul. My body feels light and sharp. I have no wad of soggy breakfast sitting like a bowling ball in my paunch. I have no caffeine short-circuiting my nerves, no sugar "high," nothing in my mouth except the sweet taste of the warm orange.

What is causing the sadness that keeps falling across me like a shadow?

Some of it might have to do with coming around a corner of a monolith and discovering a few of the students walking in a bunch toward Delicate Arch, chattering their idiot gossip and joking with each other. They have walked almost an hour, and yet they have sensed not even the tiniest suggestion of the spirit of the place. Or maybe they *have* felt it: maybe they huddle together and talk in jokes because they do not want to confront Something Out Here. I want to tell them to shut up and split up and grow up. I want to see their faces enraptured. (A grim-faced priest in a praying cathedral takes a whispering boy hard by the ear and jerks him away from his companions—but does he do it out of reverence for the place, or out of irritation with youth in general, or does he just do it because he *can,* being the public conscience with a personal ego?) I stride around them, remind them to make notes for their journals, and walk on.

~

Oh, the arch. Delicate Arch. Another ocular illusion. The class arrives and sits down all in a line, facing the arch, looking like a cackle of blackbirds on a wire. Some are taking pictures, some are taking notes, some are taking a rest, and some are taking a smoke. The arch is about a hundred yards away and looks no larger than the arches at McDonald's. It is not at all symmetrical: one side is shaped like a fat rain barrel bulging upward and breaking into a clumsy curve. The other leg is thinner and stands on a rounded rock, like a thick log balanced on a squashy basketball. It's narrow and high, like a small letter n sitting on a redstone platform. Landscape Arch soars across a gorge and has a pretty rise in the center, like a woman's upper lip when she slowly pronounces "bourbon." Delicate Arch just stands on the slickrock like it might suddenly decide to walk away down the slope.

The real illusion of Delicate Arch is in its size. From a distance, the flat basketball rock at the base of one leg seems to be perhaps the size of an average automobile, or smaller. When you get close, it turns out to be two stories high: a person standing by it looks like an ant standing next to a pomegranate. From the vantage point where the trail suddenly turns to give you your first view of the arch, you might see a person already down there. But the human height (which you know to be six feet or less) and the arch-elevation simply do not jibe. Your mind rejects the possibility of the arch being that huge and begins searching for some logical explanation.

The sun rises this morning, just as advertised in Utah tourist brochures, but after it has made a brief, white strobe flash across the sandstone through the canyon and arch formations, it vanishes behind thick low clouds. The brightness that remains behind seems not to throw any shadows. I had moved to a high place just to see it come up. But it is all right. Down in the wide sand valley below me, across a dip in the hills east of Delicate Arch, another natural amphitheater catches my attention. It looks like a concert shell, a perfect stage.

In a spontaneous fantasy, I imagine an actress rehearsing her monologue in that cavernous chamber. At center stage—a little to the left—is a pool, a rainwater pool, a little mirror reflecting two bonsai junipers that the wind has twisted dramatically. Front stage, left: a bushy juniper and two or three piñons have grown into a low curtain. And how that curvature of the back wall would throw her voice! What a worthy platform, what a fitting theater! I thought of climbing down there to try it myself. Just as I am beginning to remember a few lines from Shakespeare that I might recite on that titanic stone stage, a voice from the real world announces the departure of the group. Ah, yes. The group. I return to the trail and follow the group back toward the bus. Back through drifts of red silt we trudge, back down the gravel paths that lead through damp desert watercourses, back across slickrock space, back into bus-scheduled time.

I catch up with Tom, and we talk about students while we walk. He has been listening to a few of them during the Delicate Arch jaunt, helping them with ideas about their papers. Have any of them talked to me about those papers yet? Oh, I guess a couple of them have. The rest don't seem interested, I tell him. "Well," he replies, "sometimes you have to go after them and make them talk to you. Sometimes they don't know what really good ideas they have until you give them that little extra boost."

Maybe when we get to the Colorado and its running waters, I think. Maybe I can get in touch with the students then. There is one hopeful note, at least: I envy Tom for the easy way he has of making them do their work.

At this point, I wish I could say that those lines of Shakespeare I was thinking about earlier had some special significance. But all the significance they contained was Shakespeare's water metaphor:

> There is a tide in the affairs of men
> Which, taken at the flood, leads on to fortune;
> Omitted, all the voyage of their life
> Is bound in shallows and in miseries.
> —*Julius Caesar* 4.3.217–20

Our affairs now take us to Canyonlands, and then on to the floods of the Colorado River.

PART SIX • THE STUMBLING RUNNER AND THE SLENDER BUDDHA

Congress did well when they chose the name "Department of the Interior." The department preserves an amazing array of big and little places where you can come into contact with your interior, where you can get down into your own mental viscera and see what you have digested from life. Canyonlands is interior country. It leads you inside yourself to move slowly, to think, to wonder. This kind of landscape makes it easy to teach writing: you simply send the students out with notebooks and pencils and tell them to sit still and make notes. The quiet of the place will do the rest.

The trick to it is to sit. And keep sitting. If you must move, move slowly and walk upon the earth as if you held it sacred. Give up the madness that says you must make mileage. Our campground at Canyonlands is half-full, or half-empty. This surprises me, since we are there at the height of tourist season. But then I remember that the average American tourist is a sensible fellow. He looks in his AAA guidebook, or his mail-order park pamphlets; finds the List of Available Facilities (See Key to Symbols); and sees that Canyonlands has no swimming pool, does not offer scheduled naturalist programs, lacks souvenir shops, and does not have an air-conditioned museum. Or any museum. The logical traveler next studies the Weather to Expect section of his material: the temperature to expect is near the Fahrenheit century mark. The Canyonlands ranger tells me that he has only one reservation before September and that October is the best time to visit. By October, however, the summer tourists are back in the city, back in their *own* land of concrete canyons, busily making what they call a living.

I interrupt one of my walks to chat with a young couple camped near us. They have the right idea about this place, and they have brought along two very sensible pieces of equipment: a screen tent and a pair of bicycles. The screen tent keeps out most of the gnats and provides shade during the broiling daylight hours, and it is insurance against sudden rain squalls. But at the same time, it is not noisy and claustrophobic like the interior of a trailer or RV. The bicycles are the ideal way to see the tourist part of the park; inside an air-conditioned car is the worst way. You might as well stay home and view it on a videotape. These two people mostly sleep in the screened shade during the day's hot hours and bike around the miles and miles of paved road before sunrise and after sunset.

The moon is new tonight. As I am drifting off to sleep, I can imagine what it would be like if it were a full moon and if we—the she who is not here and I—could be gently bicycling Canyonlands' deserted asphalt paths in moonlight.

❧

When I was in high school, I had a creative writing teacher who had us write essays that began with the line "Come, take my hand and walk with me." Our imaginations had to supply the rest. Now that we are at Canyonlands, about which too much has already been written, why don't you come and walk with me and we will see what kind of interior landscapes we can discover.

The black asphalt road leads along a corridor formed by miles of natural sandstone walls and parapets. Among them, in the walls, we see frequent fissures. Canyons. Great gaping inviting cracks in the world! Tom points out several of them in particular and tells me that a hiker in this canyon or in that gully eventually will come to fresh water that runs through huge natural stone tubs and through green oases of pine and juniper trees in cool-shadowed gorges. Canyonlands National Park is, in fact, mostly off the roads. Maps and guidebooks describe the trails in terms of how steep they are, whether water is available, and which natural hazards exist on them. Beyond the trails, you find empty canyon upon canyon, mesa upon mesa, and over it all the vast empty sky.

True walkers, Thoreau says, are born and not made. *Ambulator nascitur, non fit.* If we were true walkers, and if we had the courage to follow those unknown canyons into more of the interior terrain, we might possibly walk right into Eden. Everywhere we go, there is always a place that we could have gone further into. Our life is marked by many uncompleted journeys—the author whose books we have half-read, the city that we have half-explored, the hobby we have done by halves, the trip into our own minds that remains unfinished. Someday, we tell ourselves, someday.... Looking through the bus window, I carefully memorize the shadowed entrance to one certain cleft through the redstone wall. "Let's be willing, let's come back here by moonlight," whispers my soul to me, "and walk—not run—walk backward, in this deep crack of time, to Eden."

❧

Above our camp is this rock. Or perhaps I should say that our camp sits in an erosion below one of the remaining plateaus of an ancient seafloor. Pick whichever perspective you prefer: either we will ascend from camp until we can stand on the floor of the sea, or we will climb up, high above the valley, to the peak. Perhaps the same choice of perspectives exists when you think of going into the canyons and clefts of the spirit: are you entering some place, or are you actually leaving and going out of where you have been? You should note in your journal the difference between climbing this rock formation and climbing in the Rocky Mountains. There are no trees here, no pleasant river valleys cutting the slopes, no hulking shoulders of granite cropping up like gray warts in the woods. In the tree-covered Rockies, you need to find trails through the trees and routes up around the granite cliffs. To go up this redstone rock, however, you simply start strolling, changing course just because you want to find out where this or that way will lead you. The little ledges are like sidewalks sculpted into the sandstone. You might find yourself wandering behind the mesa—eight or ten city blocks from camp—and then stepping up a few ledges to another walkway where you can walk another direction. Up another ledge, with a few easy leaps over eroded ruts, and you find that you are "up top."

Or, if you chose the other perspective on things, you have now surfaced. A half-hour ago you were down there where the geology is a million years older, and now you are standing up here on the sediment of the present epoch. You are in the present tense. (Or you are in the present, tense.)

Now, what do we see as we look back down into the past below us? There are some specks of red and blue and bright green below, in hues too unnatural to be associated with anything other than nylon—the tents of camp, down there on the ocean bottom a million years away. Near them sits an aluminum blob, a loaf-shaped metal thing that seems to be melting in the desert heat. The bus. From up here on our seafloor, there appears to be very little purpose in that bus being there. If it had feelings and could speak, it would probably say that it sees no earthly reason to be baking the life from its tires and boiling away its engine oil out here in Canyonlands where buses are too ponderous to be useful and too bulky to be hidden. The large green groves you see *are* groves—piñon or cedar—and the thin little black strip, so fragile and slender, is the road. It is either the road *into* Canyonlands, or the road *out of* Canyonlands, depending upon your inclinations. Every route will lead us in either direction, until we come to the center of our own interior journey: at that point, all roads will lead out. That's how we know we are at the center of things.

Look down to where the sandstone sidewalks widen out and become sweeping cirques and spacious courtyards, rain basins and amphitheaters.

Some of them have actual pools of actual water in them, looking like a mirage. Several of the pools, hanging halfway between the top of the mesa and the floor of the canyon, come complete with a border of red mud, a patch of grass, and a few stunted trees. Bonsai arboretums. They make romantic campsites, high on the rock. One, for example, looks quite inviting. It's just thirty yards down, directly below your protruding toes. It's as large as a backyard, and just about as level. It's made of sandstone, curved and carved and sanded into smooth contours everywhere; a small pool of water near the sidewall looks inviting, luring you away from the edge of the ledge. Cedars grow thick and short here, screening one side of this pool.

If we take a sun-bearing, we find out that this particular campsite would catch the first light of sunrise, in this season. That red sun of morning would put on its pyrotechnic display for you out there over the mesa tops, out there along that fringe of wrinkled ribbon clouds that perpetually hover at the horizon line. It would be a beautiful sunrise, coming up far out there at the edge of the land of canyons.

It would be beautiful, too, to lie there as you awakened and became conscious of daylight's stealthy approach. You would be awake early and see only black sky at first, a sky spotted with stars, a sky gradually becoming more and more blue. You would waken to the darkness, but as the light grew and the sky grew more visible, you would become aware that the cliff behind you is not black but deep red. Then you would see color in the shadowy cedar branches, as the light grew. Then the cool, pure morning air would strike you. Then the sun would appear like the edge of a shining copper disk under the crinkled ribbon clouds, like a bright arch starting to grow out of the edge of the sandworld. As it grew and grew, it would look like copper looks when it is heated to a glowing red—deep red, blood red, red as coals breaking into the fire, and disk-shaped with sharp edges.

And when you stood up, that hot copper sun would throw a long shadow against the cliff, and the shadow would be you. Your shadow would be born again to the morning light, brought fresh into a new day's world. Life-heat from the early sun would slap your face into life. Its insistence would become stronger as the long day went on.

Far out and all around us there are other mesas like ours, seemingly identical except that they are shimmering. If we were standing on one of *those*, of course, we would see that our rock shimmers, too. The canyons seem to be throbbing with heat waves; we have the feeling that the endless mornings have brought unchanging waves of heat to this slowly turning wilderness. Frank Waters wrote about this land of deep canyons in his book about the Colorado River. In order to understand it, he said, you must learn to think in terms of depth and of time, and then in terms of the eternal rather than of time. So stand here "at gaze," as Keats wrote, and make yourself feel Canyonlands in terms of depth and eternity. Someday, if you learn your lesson well, you may be able to gaze into the depths of yourself and see something eternal.

❦

In the desert, the morning sun has a way of bringing you back to reality. And the reality of it is that you are a rather small and wholly expendable life-form in the big scheme of things. Sometimes, just when we think we have things well centered and under control, something happens to remind us that we don't have all the control we would like.

My return to reality, I realize now, came when Krista got lost. Before then, I hadn't really thought about the potential for disaster that would accompany a field trip such as ours. It was a job, and a means of seeing some fine country, and my main concern was that I had been experiencing a growing alienation from the students. Up until Krista got lost, the trip had been without major accident; it was then that I realized for the first time that somebody—me, Joe, the Southwest Studies Program, Colorado College—somebody was actually responsible for deaths and kidnappings and poisonings, for encounters with axe murderers in campgrounds and botulism in the food, responsible for Being In Charge and therefore liable for all the thousand perils that are inherent in outdoor terrain, sunshine, rain, bacteria, mental defects, and gravity.

When they are in high school, adolescents derive their individuation from the familiar identity-markers of home and friends; each has an individual home and family, each belongs to a circle of adolescents and has an identity within it. But in college, where "home" is a dormitory room identical to every other concrete-block cubicle in every other university and where the circle of friends has been broken, students seek artificial ways to make their own individuality known. Out here in the West, many of the males identify themselves through their customized pickup trucks, while females adopt "personal" trademarks of dress and makeup. Both sexes are also inclined to self-identify through outdoor sports: one student is not just a student, he is a "rock climber"; another is a "cyclist" complete with the costume and full equipment; still another is a "skateboarder" first and a mere student second.

Krista was a runner. It was necessary, therefore, for her to run at Canyonlands. It was necessary for her to leave camp during the free afternoon hour, when the rest of us were writing or resting, and run. Her motives were both complex and simple. Let's just say that, being a runner, she ran. Maybe she was born a runner; maybe society made her one.

Being in the southwest desert, the Canyonlands temperature that afternoon hovered near one hundred degrees. The danger of such a climate is also both simple and complex. Heat heightens evaporation, and so does moving the body through the air; evaporation gives the illusion of coolness; the illusion of coolness leads to the illusion that the body fluids are not evaporating at a deadly rate.

Being in Canyonlands, the terrain is also deceptive. I have said that it is romantic, and it is. But it is also capable of being terrifying. Landmarks will lie to you. All of those singular-looking rock formations, such as we saw at Arches, start to look alike. Once you get into a canyon, you actually take little notice of them; you place your trust in your intuition and some kind of unconscious memory to get you back to wherever you were. But the shapes, though odd, tend to be so unalike, so consistently unique, that their uniqueness becomes commonplace; what you intended to remember as a landmark, that freak formation, gets lost in a crowd of freaks.

We had set up camp and were taking the midafternoon break. The appointed team of cooks was actually preparing a real supper; I think it was to be Mystery Macaroni Mess and Scrap Salad. Krista went out to run before eating.

Now that I think about it, Krista's adventure really sums up one of Canyonlands' dangerous temptations. You must ride in a car or in a bus, and ride a long, long way to get there. And when you are finally set loose, all you see is a desert-and-stone wonderland that seems to go on forever; muscle-cramped from your long trip, you experience an overpowering urge to walk or run or climb a rock. Everyone does it: a few minutes after they leave the bus, everyone is wandering up onto the rocks, or out along the sandy flat corridors in between. Anything rather than sit still. I can picture Krista, eager to leave the campsite, stretching out, halfheartedly helping her tent-mates select a place to put up the tent, looking off down that empty road while she carried gear from the bus to the camp.

Soon she broke away; she was out on the road, alone at last; she began to jog gradually, with exaggerated slowness at first. Then as soon as she felt the rhythm of arms and legs starting to come together, as her muscles started to respond to her will with pliable elastic energy, she felt swift and light, and was off on her late afternoon run.

She ran on, runningonrunningonrunningon, breathing deeply but not laboriously, her legs losing the loping-gazelle feeling and settling down into a measured stride; when she left the blacktop for a narrow sandy road, she felt the sand requiring an extra little push at the ankle with each stride and she made that part of her measured stride and ran on across the sand. She came to a turn and took it and was running alongside a mesa that was five miles long and towered eight hundred feet above her. To the eyes of the swallow who had just ridden a rising thermal over the eight hundred–foot parapet, she was a miniature figure, barely seeming to move. Her running took her to a straight streak of sand through clumpy brush and lumpy rocks. The swallow banked and pivoted in slow motion; below him, the tiny girl turned again. Now she ran along a narrow sandwash that led straight into another canyon. If the swallow cared to think about it, he would have been able to see where she was headed. She could run through that canyon to the other end, curve to her left and cross over a low pinkish dune, then bend to the right and cross a dune directly ahead of her, descend the wind-formed crescent sandhill by the stone outcrop, and so reach her original road again.

The swallow, from his swallow-eye view, could also have seen something else, something that Krista was not able to see from her earthbound perspective: the gorges of Canyonlands stretch all the way from one hazy horizon to the faraway purple mountains. Mile upon century they stretch, all those stone citadels and storm-washed moats, like skyscraping monoliths, like open subway trenches in the eternal gloom of stone shadows, fathoms and leagues of gargantuan mesas and gorges that gape like a person holding her breath after a yawn.

Krista's breath was hot and dry in her throat. But her respiration was still deep and steady. Beginning to feel hot. Soon each breath would seem like the blast from a blowtorch shooting up the airtube from her lungs. The fiery heat of her breath seemed to hover at her lips; now, each time she inhaled, she seemed to be inhaling the same heat and the same air over and over. She began to think about sweat; she could feel it on her forehead and wondered why it was not running on down into her eyes. She did not mind, because she had left her sweatband back at camp and was glad that the sweat was not running down into her eyes. She did not realize the reason: in the desert heat, it was evaporating first.

Back at camp, I was sucking the juice of a pre-supper orange and writing some notes about the local geology.

By the time Krista realized that she had missed her landmark—and now had no idea where camp was—she knew that she was in a geological and physical trap. She could see the sun, now low on the horizon, and so she could figure out her directions; what she could not determine was the direction in which camp lay. If she stayed down in the canyon floor, she could never hope to spot any remembered landmark; if she climbed up one of those sandstone giants, she might see a landmark, but it would mean an expenditure of her dwindling energy and might be just a waste of the diminishing daylight. She could save energy by slowing down to a walk as she looked for the road, but then the darkness might catch her out there in that maze of rocks. She could go on running and thereby cover more ground, but it would be at the cost of what little body moisture she had left.

Krista was discovering something that is, in the abstract, rather wonderful. At a place as wild as Canyonlands, time, place and personality all become insignificant. You are alone, anonymous and unnecessary. You are never exactly sure where anything is in relation to your Self. You are never exactly sure how long you have been there, or how long you can afford to stay.

At camp, supper over, I threw a scrap of bread to a scavenging raven. He was a huge, black embodiment of darkness who had found out that it was easier to beg from humans than to circle the canyons with the turkey buzzards in hopes of spotting some doomed flesh crawling along the hot sand below. I washed down my own piece of bread with some warm canteen water and poured the rest over my shirt. I could get more water at the tap.

Krista came to a hardpacked sand road and managed to pant a smile. She even grinned a little as she stumbled. Camp soon. The road. Her road. Looking left and right for the campground. Could miss it, back in the brush. Back in the cool of the curved rock wall. See the bus, though. Can't miss the bus. Good or smelly big bus. Watch for bus.

Krista labored along that road with all of her remaining energy, convinced that she was soon going to be back among friends, back where water and food were waiting. But then, before she had gone a mile, something about that road suddenly dawned on her. No footprints. No imprints of a measured stride pushing soft sand back from the ball of the foot with a slight trick of the ankle; that confident runner (had it been she who ran like that, so easily and well?) had not passed this way.

I read her journal later, and it gave only a sketchy, foggy account of her feelings at that point. She was unsure of what actually happened next, but she and I talked about it. When she didn't show up for supper, I was worried. Everyone was worried. And when she finally arrived, just as we were getting out the flashlights for a search party, something happened between us. She was no longer just another student. I was no longer the professor. She ate and drank and rested, and we talked far into the evening about her experience. I can tell you how she came to find the camp again. She gave herself up to the canyon. She stopped trying to figure out her directions, stopped worrying about exhaustion and daylight, and simply went on running.

At the Picuris pueblo a few years ago, my wife and I watched young people running their annual "race" with the sun. From the sun comes their energy: to express their respect for that sacred energy, they run back and forth on a trail laid out between the points of sunrise and sunset until all of their own energy has been returned to the sun. It is a simple and sacred and beautiful expression of how well they understand the relationship of themselves to the sun and the meaning of the sun to all of life.

Krista surrendered herself as if she meant to sacrifice all she had to the Spirit of the Place. Perhaps she could save her life thereby, but a pure surrender of the self is seldom done with the idea of getting anything back. Maybe we should say that she simply went on running, unthinking, yielding the final quivering bit of energy in her young body to the unwavering ancient power in the rock and sand; she became one with the direction of the place and came full circle back to us in the manner of the desert. All things, finally, come back in the circle.

Was it instinct? Was it a strange subconscious conjunction of mind and landscape? If you do not agree with either of those possibilities, I have another explanation. This one might seem more logical to you, more concrete.

With her eyes dimmed and blurred by fatigue, in the dim light of dusk, Krista looked upward, but not quite high enough to see the turkey buzzards. She saw that dome-shaped sandstone formation behind our camp. It looked like St. Peter's dome, except that it has ledges encircling it. As I have pointed out, however, all of these domes tend to look alike, especially in the twilight. And this one would have looked just like any other stone dome, except for one thing: sitting upon the very summit of it, cross-legged, sitting there like a statue of Buddha facing the last bronze gleams of the dying sun, was an apparition. I saw it, too. While we were worrying about the lost girl and getting gear together to search for her, I was also worried about Tom. He, too, was missing, and this was starting to look like a crisis. Far up there on the dome, there was a slim human figure sitting in the position of meditation.

Is it possible, I wonder, for a meditating soul, sitting at guru-height on a desert rock, to know that another human spirit was experiencing fright and fatigue? As her pounding terror gave clumsy impetus to her burning feet, out there on that unmarked track of sand, could it be that some kind of intangible homing signal brought the runner back to camp?

I have stood in the gloom behind air traffic controllers and watched green dots on a screen. The controllers send signals and the dots change direction. Blindly and without question, a pilot with two hundred people in his charge hears the signal and turns his aircraft. The signal brings him home. I have heard it said that ocean whales also hear navigation signals, coming from other whales on the opposite limits of the sea. I have felt drawn by signals coming from the Thompson Canyon tragedy.

Whatever force it was that brought her, Krista came back. Her desert lesson summed up Canyonlands for me: it is big, it is impersonal, it is deceptive, and it is beautiful. It is also mystical; I believe that it is one of those sacred places on earth, a keystone in the arch of time, where humans experience a reality that is beyond ordinary dimensions, outside known measurements of time, and above the reach of sense.

✂

Too soon, it becomes time to walk down from the rock, back down through the geologic layers of time. On the floor of the ancient ocean, we fold the tents and police the area and get back into Harold's bus. We settle down in our seats to be driven a measurable distance in a determinable direction. After a period of time we will be at the next scheduled stopping place.

Someday I must go back, for I failed to confront the real spirit of place in Canyonlands. I would like to become a walker there. I would like to look it straight in the face in the worst kind of weather, like John Muir confronting his Yosemite. I would like to get face-to-face with my own human urges and hates and loves, like Abbey at Arches. I want to sit quietly and try to see it, the way Mary Austin sat and waited for the life of Death Valley to reveal itself to her. I would like to understand how Everett Ruess entered it never to be seen again. I am not anxious: to return to a place such as Canyonlands is inevitable. Someday it will simply happen that I will be back. Like the floods and droughts in Austin's little book, each happening will find its own best season.

PART SEVEN • THE MIGHTY RIVER TO MOAB

My first full-time teaching position was at a small college in southern Utah, where I was one of three or four Gentiles among a hundred-member faculty. The rest of the faculty belonged to the Church of Jesus Christ of Latter-day Saints. Lacking most of the qualifications for sainthood, I had become, for the first time ever, a minority person. My friends back in Colorado kidded me about it: according to them, I was on a two-year mission to convert the Mormons to alcohol and tobacco. They saw me, they said, going from door to door with a box of panatelas under my arm and a can of Coors in my hand.

Up until that time, I had taken my Gentile religion pretty much for granted. In fact, I had gone to church mostly as a token gesture, and while there had done my share of sneering at the "hypocrites" I saw in the other pews. But down in that little college, where almost all of my colleagues, not to mention 90 percent of the student body, were of another faith, I discovered that I had a defensive feeling toward my own religion. Faced with the possibility of losing it there, I began to truly examine and appreciate it. It was there in Utah, for example, where I finally learned that the Order of Worship had both a tradition and a meaning; up until then, for instance, I had wondered why we took up the congregational offering *after* the sermon rather than *before*. What if people decided that the sermon wasn't worth the money? Presbyterian logic, overruled by ritual. At Canyonlands, unexpectedly faced with the real possibility that we had lost a student, I discovered my own capacity for caring. In that brief hour of uncertainty, I let go of my desire to be somewhere else, and with someone else, and accepted the role for which I had signed the contract. I became responsible, not only for the girl's physical safety, but responsible to her need to tell someone about the strangeness of the whole experience. It is an old truth, but a truth nonetheless, that we seem not to appreciate something until we are faced with losing it.

The emergency is over, we will lose no more students, and we are on our way to get wet in the Colorado at last! Finally, we are going to get into small boats and place ourselves at the mercy of the gods of the moving waters.

The bus hums with anticipation as we drive toward Moab, where the river guides await us. None of the students has been on white water before. Neither have I. We share a sense of apprehension, although we cover it with excited chatter about what the trip will be like. Tom has considerable experience with rubber boats and rapids, and we have hundreds of questions for him. If you are thrown from the boat, is it best to go down the rapids feet first, or try to bodysurf the torrent? How many have drowned in this stretch of the wild Colorado River? What if the paddles are lost—would it be best to try to swim for shore, or let the current carry the boat toward unseen dangers below? If the last boat in line overturns, how will the rest of them be able to come back up the river to the rescue? What if you don't swim very well? Will the life jackets protect you against the rocks, once you are caught in the white water?

The answers are not elaborate, nor are they encouraging. In fact, they can be summed up in four words: Stay in the Boat. This is going to be excitement. And I do not mind admitting now that it carried with it so much that was unknown and potentially dangerous that I think I might not have gone through with it had it not been for the pressure of the group at the time. I could remain at the pickup point, I reason, or even in Moab, while the class goes and has fun. But when I look into a few individual faces and see there the same apprehension that *I* am concealing in myself, I know that there is no going back. With four boats of rank amateurs and one experienced river-runner, I am going to hurl myself down the Colorado.

If you ever wonder whether you have lost your youth, plan an adventure. In so doing, if a sense of fear and anticipation hones the edge of your imagination, if there is a simultaneous reluctance and eagerness, if there is a persistent curiosity about the unknown aspects of your adventure, then you have not lost it.

When you actually begin moving toward that experience, you will undergo a certain change of mind. Your imagination will grow. Back near the turn of this century, Frederick Jackson Turner listed several traits of mind he had observed as being characteristic of Americans, and he postulated that it was the presence of a frontier on the American continent that had "called forth" those traits. Among them was imagination. If you have ever launched yourself out toward a personal frontier where your accustomed habits will be insufficient, your imagination becomes as alert and sensitive as an exposed nerve.

Take Moab, for instance. It is an ordinary small town, founded as the Elk Mountain Mission by Mormon colonists back in 1855. According to Faun M. Tanner's *History of Moab,* it then became known as Grand Valley, because it controlled access to a crossing of the Grand—now Colorado River; then, in good Mormon fashion, a committee was formed to rename the town, preferably with a biblical name such as Enoch or Ephraim, Goshen or Zion. If you look at an Old Testament map of the Bible lands, you will see that there is a city and a kingdom called Moab, lying south and east of the Dead Sea, between the sea and the desert. In 1881 the committee came up with the same name, Moab, for this town that lies south and east of the Great Salt Lake and west of the desert.

At least one local joker will tell you, however, that the name comes from the Indian word *moapa*—mosquito. I have not seen the Old Testament kingdom, but I have seen Mormon mosquitoes, and therefore I will keep an open mind. As a matter of fact, it is in anticipation of the mosquitoes and gnats that I am going into town to find a repellent—and will soon end up with my imagination running at high speed. I am "wired," as the students say, for this raft trip on the Colorado; even before the bus comes to a full halt on the Moab side street, I am out of my seat and anxious to be done with the shopping and on with the trip.

My imagination is really flying. Each Moabite I see going in and out of the supermarket looks like an interesting character to use in a short story; inside this small "super" market there is a smell of ripe cantaloupe and cardboard boxes. The odors hovering around the grind-your-own coffee machine seem as exotic as Persian spice. The place is filled with the low hum of humanity. I am in a hurry and stay only long enough to buy some candy bars and some film (and some cigars, in case I run into a missionary opportunity). But in those few minutes inside the store, I think it is the best, the most charming, the most intriguing supermarket I have seen in years.

One by one and two by two, our group drifts through town, looking for ways to spend an hour while Joe "El Jefe" Gordon arranges for the rafts and guides. I need some bug lotion, and so it is that I wander into the principal drugstore of Moab—possibly the only drugstore of Moab—and step back into 1955. It has a soda fountain! An honest-to-vanilla soda fountain! The instant I come in the door, I smell that light, creamy scent of places where fresh milk is kept. I smell the sweet syrup smell of cherry cola. I smell malted milk and chocolate ice cream! even though I am still at the front of the store where my olfactory nerves are being assaulted by cedarwood Souvenirs of Moab and gift boxes of fruit-scented soap next to the eau de Walgreen perfume counter.

I walk back through the drugstore to see if it is true. It is. Do you remember sitting high on those wobbly revolving stools, the kind with the thick seats that are covered in sticky vinyl of a color that can never be named, and leaning forward with your elbows on the cool linoleum countertop, watching that malt mixer make your malt? The dull avocado-green motor, sort of bulb-shaped, grinding away, the long blades whirring and thickening the mixture, the stainless-steel cup starting to get frosty on the outside? Did you unconsciously lick your lips when the swoosh, swoosh sound turned to swoooooooooosh as your malted milk reached the culmination of its being, and did your tongue roam the inside of your mouth, looking for the first cold flavor of malt and milk and chocolate powder?

The Moab fountain girl is pretty and young, as all of them used to be and should be, and she knows the ritual to perfection. She makes a tantalizing, dramatic production out of pouring my malt from the frosty steel cup into the waiting glass, letting it ooze over the metal rim so slow, slow, slow . . . when it has heaped up in the glass, she smiles and winks and leaves the cup there on the counter, a little malt running down and mingling with the condensation to make a brownish puddle on the green countertop. Inside the mixing cup, the remaining chocolate malt is gradually sliding down to collect in the bottom; I will slurp up that little leftover bit later, like dessert. As I sit there waiting, I even reexperience my boyhood curiosity about malted milk mixing. I have not thought about these things in thirty years. Why is it that the tall, fancy serving glasses *never* hold as much malted milk as the steel mixing cup? Why is there always an inch or so left in the bottom? Why do straws make a slurping sound? How does the mixer know to turn itself on when the cup is pushed into place, and how does it know to turn off when the mixture is thick?

It is a simple wonderment, and a precious one, as I sit passing the time at the soda fountain. It is enough wonder for me. Without doubt, I could find even more magic sights in Moab; however, I will have to discover them some other day. The hour has passed, the group drifts back to the bus, and it is time. The steel doors slam shut with an ominous finality, and, like mythical Charon casting off from the shore of the Styx, Harold draws the bus away from the curb and starts toward the edge of town. We have twenty miles of dirt road to cover, twenty miles to appreciate the safe, comfortable seats of our good ol' Goodwill Greyhound. Twenty miles to our rendezvous with the rubber boats.

☙

When Major John Wesley Powell and his nine companions ran the Colorado River in 1869, there was only one type of boat to be seen on the river. They were wooden rowboats, there were only four of them, and Powell's party had them all. Today you can find jet boats, airboats, canoes, kayaks and inflatables.

There are three common species of inflatables inhabiting the Colorado. They lie dormant most of the winter months, but as the weather gets warm and the water begins to rise you can expect to see hatches of them occurring almost anywhere there is a road down to the water. They begin in clusters, then venture out into deeper water, and begin their summer-long life as aquatic fauna. As the water drops in the fall, they begin a ritual of bumping and slamming into one another as if trying to mate; then, on a given day when certain rocks appear above the waterline, they return to their winter resting places.

Other than their shared behavioral habits, the various species of inflatables have little in common with each other. They tend to remain in groups of their own kind, and violent waterfights have been known to break out when one group is rash enough to venture into the territory of another. The largest (but least aggressive) type rides on enormous pontoons; the passengers sit on a kind of excursion-bus seating arrangement. This boat goes over the rapids easily: from shore, it looks like a duo of lethargic sausages tied together, panting and heaving themselves up the upriver side of a river wave and then sliding down the downriver side with a fatalistic sigh. The sausage-pontoons go through all sorts of grotesque distortions, absorbing the shock and energy of the churning water and keeping the people relatively comfortable. The people hold on and talk and laugh and take pictures. The second sort of inflatable, in order of size, is a giant life raft. It has a wooden platform across the middle; here sits the bronze, muscular "river driver," gripping a pair of long oars. From his throne-chair he rows the life raft and keeps up a monologue of clever sayings. The passengers sit in an oval formation around his feet; they grip the handropes and the rubber and each other. They laugh nervously at the clever sayings, unless they are in the clutch of the white water. Then they scream.

Being shorter and having a flat bottom rather than a pair of pudgy keels, this type of boat does not ooze over the standing waves like a pontoon boat. Instead, it climbs up and up the upriver side of a wave until half of its length—and half of its passengers—hang out in empty air, suspended over the water. Then the raft bends at the middle, as if making a formal bow. Possibly it is just trying to look down and see where the bottom of the trough is. There is a second of hesitation, and then it decides to slip down between the mountainous waves. The sensation is like riding a hockey puck down the slope of an iceberg. The people who ride these rafts do not take pictures.

Our rafts are smaller. Three people on each side, and a steersman in back. The paddles we hold are functional, not just stage props. We have to paddle, and paddle hard, so that our raft will be driven up the back of each wave; because the thing is short and relatively light, it could stall out on the way up that incline. And if it does, its front end will be pointing almost straight up and the rear end will be stuck down at the bottom of the trough below, and the boat will do one of two things. Either it will fill with water or it will fall toward one side. If it fills with water and becomes stern-soggy, the two people forward will fall backward into the laps of the persons behind them. Domino effect. This *will* cause the boat to turn over; when the bow is suddenly lightened and the stern suddenly gains weight, the latter is swept under the former like a kid somersaulting between his own legs.

If the stalled raft manages to rise and get its front end airborne and then falls off to one side (because *someone* was not paddling hard enough), the people who were on the high side come avalanching over the people on the low side and the raft turns turtle. If you prefer doing this maneuver rather than the somersault, the physics of it are quite simple: find the fat person who cannot paddle fast and put him on one side, then put a light, fast paddler on the other. With any sort of decent wave at all, your raft should go up, stall, angle off toward the fat person, and do the turtle thing.

In a lake this would be fun, flipping a rubber raft by filling it half full of water and overloading either the side or the stern. In a river such as the Colorado, where the raft moves away after dumping you, you find yourself in white water punctuated with granite, water against which you cannot swim. The first or second time you capsize, you tend to take it rather seriously. As you get further experience at it, you lose the tendency to become paralyzed and can accomplish some rather dedicated screaming. After you have been dumped at the top of eight or ten rapids and have had the following rafts run over you five or six times, paralysis and screaming finally turn into sheer hilarity. Spectators watching from the shore often mistake this hilarity for hysteria.

Between dunkings, you are expected to stay in the raft and follow certain procedures. You sit sidesaddle on the puffy, pneumatic sides, with your legs inside (protruding river rocks have a nasty way of breaking tibias and pulverizing patellas). You paddle. You need both hands on the paddle to be an effective paddler, which leaves you with no way to get a suitable death grip on the plunging wet rubber under your butt. On one particularly sporty stretch of river, I developed a technique called "grab-handrope-balance-paddle-twice-grab-rope-paddle-grab." A paddle lost to the river costs ten bucks, and I took note of the fact that the outfitter collected her ten bucks *in advance*. The rest of the procedure (for those who choose to remain inside the raft) is simple: paddle like crazy and scream and ride the bucking oval doughnut right to the crest of each wave and all the way to the bottom of every trough. Most photographs you see of the six-person raft in action have been taken from shore.

~

We arrive at the launch site and find four inflated rafts and two nearly naked guides waiting for us. Like the waters of the Colorado seeking their own level, each student gravitates toward a group that is to his or her liking. Then the groups mill around, wondering what to do next. I share the feeling: I don't know whether to go sit in one of the beached rafts and wait for orders, or to start some kind of orderly launch drill, or to just get back in the bus.

Tom, you recall, has experience with river-running. Being experienced and being a responsible teacher, he quickly commandeers one of the rafts and impresses six of us into service as propulsion power. His choices make good sense (although at the time I did not have time to fully appreciate it): two professors (El Jeffe and myself), two football players named Mike and Matthew, Krista, and an equally athletic young lady named Amy. While the other raft crews mill about on the beach or struggle to get their vessel into the water, we wade ours out into the current, jump in, and start paddling. We christen our craft Prof Boat Number One.

The sole mission of Prof Boat Number One, Tom explains, is to stay in the lead. It is a race, and he explains that either we will win or he will keelhaul the entire crew. Right behind us as we push off the beach is what we call Muffy Boat Number Two. One of the Greek-god river guides sits at the helm of that craft, and for his motivating force he has an assortment of awestricken students. He has an air of command and he knows the river. But besides an experienced (and merciless) steersman, we have a secret weapon: two football players powering our bow paddles. Front-end drive. Tom places the two girls in the middle, where their light weight and quick strength will give us better maneuverability. He orders the two professors into the stern seats. I presume that his reason for doing this is to get our cool courage, our steadiness under pressure, our maturity back where it can do the most good. Later I discover that he actually did it so that the students wouldn't see the terror in our faces and become disheartened.

Number Three is dubbed the Animal Boat. It has no guide and no one firmly in command. It is paddled by a wholly unorganized bunch of ruffians, each yelling his own orders and each paddling in a different direction. Between their meandering trips from shore to shore, while attempting to keep the raft somewhere in the river, and their series of spectacular capsizings, these students see more of the river than anyone else—often from the bottom of it looking up. Finally, far to the rear of our flotilla, comes the Greenhorn Boat. The steersman takes it upon himself to stay far behind the other craft so that his crew can retrieve our lost paddles, yell encouragement to swimmers who have been thrown from the Animal Boat, and practice correct paddling technique. The Greenhorn contains one river guide, a statistically correct mixture of males and females, refreshments, dry clothing, extra paddles, and (I wouldn't be surprised) at least two waterproof Bibles.

There is a certain feeling that comes with river-running, and you might as well know right now that I cannot describe it. From the launch to the landing, your adrenaline churns up your blood sugar. I laugh hilariously. I tense up until my neck is in a knot. I relax to the point of being nonchalant. I shout, I fly.

Here comes a rapid: I can hear it coming—even over the shouts of the waterfight going on between boats—a faraway roaring as if a train were coming up the canyon. It is the big-chested laboring rumble of a diesel crawling steadily under an uphill load; it echoes like long, dull thunder against the high canyon walls. The water of the river, the surface, has become slick. Calm. *Too* calm. Ominously calm. Stretching my neck so I can see without standing up, I can see ahead to where the rapids start. There is one strange phenomenon about this that I never get used to: I can *hear* the power of suddenly falling water as it slams into rocks and crashes over itself; but, sitting only a few feet above the river's surface, the only thing I can really *see* is a line of riffles waiting for us. Just tiny, innocent little ripples, shining serene in the bright sun. Past that deceptive little washboard, the river disappears wholly from view; I can see it again much further downstream; the part just ahead has become invisible, out of sight.

What is *in* that invisible part? And we drift toward it, slowly easing the boat along with light strokes, not anxious to find out. Then the edge comes closer. We all have the urge, I think, to paddle backward. I try to swallow hard, but the gulp gets hung up halfway down my throat; we have passed the go-no-go point now: even with frantic paddling, we could not angle to the shore in time to miss these rapids. Imagine it. You are facing oblivion; you are in the first boat to go down; and your safety is in the hands of a steersman who has never before seen these rapids.

I develop a routine: as we approach each set of rapids I stretch to see what is ahead, then go back to paddling and wondering which level of Dante's Hell is waiting under the rim of the water, and then I calculate the last possible moment at which I can leap out of the raft and swim for shore. As soon as that opportunity for safety is lost—forever—and the raft is committed to the rapids, I wedge one foot under the inflated seat ahead of me, get a white-knuckle grip on my ten-dollar paddle, and put my trust in Tom.

I'll say this for Tom as a boat captain: he is democratic. He offers us choices at each set of falls. The choices, however, remind me of the choice my grandfather used to offer us at the dinner table when he waved the bowl of mashed potatoes past us and asked, "Anybody *except me* want any of this?" and naturally no one did. Tom says, "Okay, shall we go down the tongue where it's smooth, or shall we head for the heavy water? Maybe take a chance that the big swell over there isn't hiding an even bigger rock? Okay, who would like to see the hole behind this next boulder?"

Have *you* ever seen a "hole" up close? From a thin rubber boat? A hole. Some hole. The entire Colorado River pounds down a hard slope, steep as a staircase, boiling and roiling reddish-brown-and-white foam and roaring, and it throws itself into collision against a boulder the size of a house. A portion of the river goes on over the top, just enough to carry a light raft halfway across the stone. The bulk of the river splits; it goes rushing around both sides of the huge obstruction and comes crashing together again on the downriver side, leaving a water-rimmed "hole" in the river. Some holes are merely nuisances, just temporary traps that grab and hold a rubber boat in their suction. But *other* holes—Harold could stand our Trailways bus on end in some of them and you would not see it from shore. If you fall into one of *those* "holes," friend, instead of wishing that you could photograph the experience, you can start writing out a check to cover seven paddles, one raft and a memorial service.

Prof Boat Number One goes merrily on its way for the first few miles, pounding and slapping and bucking as Tom deliberately steers us through the most violent section of each set of rapids. As we climb the high-standing waves and tilt and careen down them again, screaming and paddling like maniacs, it occurs to me that the calm person sitting in the stern with the steering paddle *is* mostly metaphysical. That fact seems to explain his choice of routes through the rapids but does very little to reassure those of us who happen to believe that the preservation of one's physical body is pretty much essential to continued existence.

To give yourself a sketchy idea of what it is like to run the Colorado rapids, you should first imagine being absolutely surrounded by walls of water. If you are sitting in a room right now, and the room has walls—well, there's your watery prison. Now imagine that your chair is carrying you steadily toward one of those liquid walls, and that you know that you are about to actually ride *up* it—sitting down. That is our situation when we hit the rock. The river has taken a long curve toward the cliffs on our right. We have oozed over the lip of a slick stretch and down into a series of "haystack" moguls. The raft flexes and heaves as we come to the high-walled standing waves; we go over one of them at an angle, tilted alarmingly, slide down to the bottom, and are looking up at the moving liquid walls all around us.

We paddle hard, forgetting to hold on, keeping our balance in the raft by the thrust of the paddles in the water, forcing the raft up onto the steep back of the next huge wave. And it is huge, we find, because it is flowing over a huge rock.

By this time, I am on both knees in the bottom of the raft, still trying to paddle, although I have been thrown off my seat, and when the rock smacks the rubber I feel sure it has fractured my shin.

There is no time to think about it: Amy, who was seated ahead of me, is going over the side. With more than half the force of the Colorado River exploding against the rock and with the raft in definite danger of swamping, it does not seem to be a very opportune moment for her to leave us. Nor does it appear to be something she has given much thought to. It is like a movie moving in slow motion: I see her mouth drop open, then see her arm fly upward, sending the paddle high into the air; one of her feet is still wedged under the inflatable seat and she is falling over backward into the water head down, windmilling her arms and getting smashed by the waves that are swamping the raft's gunwales and Mike grabs for her from his forward position and I jump to grab her too and our weight should turn the boat turtle but somehow a wave catches under us *just* right and she is back in the raft.

As soon as there is an opportunity, we eddy out and beach ourselves, turning the raft over to dry it out and sprawling on the sand to catch our breath. Amy's paddle caught in the eddy, so we managed to save her ten dollars. I keep asking her if she is okay, and she describes her version of the experience. I urge her to put it into her journal and make an essay of it, later on. In her version, the surprise of losing her balance and the sudden breath-stopping fear of leaving the boat and the realization of how deadly the rapids were all came at once, and then she seemed to be flying backward and then both of her arms were grabbed and she blinked and was back in the raft. I tell her it was just one of those out-of-neoprene experiences that people have sometimes, and we laugh together until the others are ready to get up and pour water on us.

El Jeffe decides that we should wait there on the beach for the Animal Boat, the Muffy Boat, and the Greenhorn to catch up. He wants a head count of survivors, since it could affect our supper arrangements.

While waiting, I make a discovery. A little further down this beach, a sandbar runs quite a distance out into the river. The opaque water is ankle-deep there, but on either side the bottom drops off suddenly to a depth of six or eight feet. As I stand there at the end of this sandbar, cooling my feet, around the upstream bend in the river comes the Muffy Boat. The Animals have finally ended up with five in the water and one in the raft, so the Greenhorns have stopped to render assistance. Muffy has come through unscathed. Even undamp. They took the gentle routes, all of them sitting well in order, all looking dry and nicely groomed and calm. They look like a collection of yuppies posing for the spring fashion issue of *New Young Collegiate*.

I look at my crew, sprawled on the sand. Some have scrapes, most have blisters. Hats and sandals have been lost. They look sandblasted and sunburned and disheveled. They are beach litter. Detritus. Flotsam and jetsam. I love them. I look again at the spic-and-span crew of the Muffy. We *definitely* have too much contrast in this picture. Somebody has to do something.

"Hey!" I yell. "Come on down here and throw me your line!"

They look doubtful, but still innocent.

"You'll have to get your shorts wet over there! Come on down here! Look, it's only ankle-deep here!"

They come. I catch their bowline and hold the raft tight for them. I keep it centered on the narrow sandbar. Naturally, they are all careful to stow their paddles under the seats, then carefully arrange their clothing. Then two of them step out into eight feet of water. Better yet, they grab the raft as they go down, throwing everyone else in the drink as well. The slovenly crew of the Prof Boat sends up a guffaw you could have heard in Moab: the ensuing waterfight is a joy to behold. I soon find myself among the walking wounded, a flying water bucket having left me with a red forehead stripe that nicely complements the purple-and-blue bruise on my swollen shin.

Joseph Wood Krutch once addressed himself to the question of human awareness, and that is what our short day on the Colorado River has been all about. Awareness. "The true beginnings of a self," he wrote, happen when an individual evolves to "some awareness of the world outside himself." Before arriving at the river, you see, it was I who was the Muffy. It was I who was proper and superior and living inside myself. But rivers do move mountains and have their ways of leveling differences.

The river trip was shouting and being drenched. It was drifting and marveling at the sheer canyon walls cut by the Colorado River. It was seeing a western grebe on a little patch of calm water; it was looking and looking for the bus waiting at the take-out point and sort of hoping we would miss it and be able to go on and on until after dark, and it was kidding and it was waterfights and mock battles, and it was pure excitement. The river served to reduce life to the basic simplicity of being one of six human beings willingly trapped together in a plunging raft. The best way to see this river, to paraphrase Thoreau, would be to simplify, simplify, and paddle as if you were fleeing hell in a leaking canoe.

I have said that I must go back alone to confront the Canyonlands again. But I do not feel any need to deepen my acquaintance with this powerful section of the Colorado River—at least, not alone. There are stories of men who have so faced it, not in fun but in earnest, and have come back from it with their sanity in serious doubt. She can be an easy river, glad to give you joy in the easy rapids. But I know, too, that there are places where her strength is clumsy and enormous and can do injury. A person would do well to study places where the river has been; he should contemplate the sandstone and the schist, the granite and the obdurate, the marble and the gneiss through which the Colorado has cut, and he should remember that the preacher says we are made of clay.

I go away from the river, although I find excuses to linger near the boats as they are being loaded, loath to leave. I go away and, like all the others, let Harold ferry me across to Colorado Springs again. The bus seems anxious to get back and whizzes over the hard highway like a Friday schoolboy going home. I am going away from rivers of snow and rivers of crystal and rivers of silt, away from rivers of dry, hot sand where ancient oceans went running down the land even while the land was being lifted up. I come away a few centuries wiser.

The river, I think as we drive through the late-night valleys, the river right now is moving no faster than it did when we were watching it. It is moving no slower than it did; it is still coming down off its mountains and still shouldering the rocks aside, still moving even as we drive, moving even as we sleep, moving like time itself, "carrying the spinal fluid of the continent," as Frank Waters says, moving no matter what we do, and moving whether we mortals pause to think about it or not, taking the innumerable sands to the unfathomable ocean and returning in shapes of mist to the continent's divide in an infinite, incomprehensible cycle.

EPILOGUE

On full-moon nights, the Mexicans say, after the spring rains, when the ghost of the river is swollen and cold and the tides are running high, the river reaches the sea again.

The river and the sea rise, black and silver in the moon. A mountain of water rolls in off the Sea of Cortez, drowning the nameless islands, the barren continents of mud and sand: rolls

> up the channel of the old river in the moonlight. Green herons rise from their nests in the thickets, making music like dull wooden bells. . . .
>
> And then the waters turn, and with a tremendous silver noise the river rushes out to sea again, streaming out into the Sea of Cortez.
>
> —Rob Schultheis, *The Hidden West*

Rob Schultheis confirms in his 1982 book, *The Hidden West*, what Frank Waters predicted in *The Colorado* in 1946. Dammed for irrigation and dammed for power and dammed for political power and dammed for human "recreation" and damned, I suspect, simply because there are such things as engineers and because one occupation of engineers is to dam things, the Colorado River never reaches the sea. She who offers rainbow dramas to high-country fishermen, she who opens her gorges for those wishing to see the history of her geology, she who carries lilliputian boaters on her bosom through gargantuan canyons—she is finally denied access to her mother, the sea.

The river itself, if it were capable of thinking, would probably be unconcerned about this. All water, after all, eventually becomes humidity and so finds its way back again to the watersheds, even without reaching the sea. Somewhere far in the future, the idea of river engineering—and possibly all civilization—may become only a dim memory of the empty earth, when the Colorado erodes away the concrete artifacts of our technology and goes flowing to the sea again.

Having briefly experienced, near Moab, how that deluge will feel and look when the canyon-running Colorado breaks free, I wanted to go and have a look at where this geological cataclysm will begin.

The process itself will come from a gradually developing series of events. First event: a small diversion structure will become choked with silt, and no one will care enough to clear it. A few more feet-per-minute will stay in the river. Second event: a hydroelectric dam will develop a slowly seeping leak down next to the bedrock, and the power company will quietly save themselves the cost of fixing it ("what with that new nuclear plant and all . . ."). More feet-per-minute. Decades will pass. A farm supply ditch will silt up, but the farm will be a subdivision by then and the ditch will have become an untidy habitat for raccoons, squirrels, muskrats, kingfishers, ducks, crawdads, minnows, reeds, insects, wild grass, cottonwoods, and such other nuisances that subdivided urbanophiles would rather do without.

Every little foot of water per second of time will have a compounding effect upon the flow and the erosion, and one day there will be too little demand and too much supply: one of the major dams will be breached. The Colorado will then quickly cut and smash her way through the rest of them and will find her old channel to the sea once again.

During the past few years, I have gone looking for river confluences, those intriguing spots on the map where two flows of water join into one. I followed the Rio Grande from its birth-mountains in Colorado down to its concrete ditch at Juárez, Mexico. I went across Texas, taking in the Pecos, the Brazos, the San Antonio, Nueces, and Sabine Rivers. At New Orleans I headed up alongside the Mississippi to the Arkansas River confluence and took the Arkansas back home to Colorado. Along my way I would ask people where these rivers came from, and where they met other rivers.

Six miles from the Arkansas/Mississippi confluence, even the staff at an Arkansas visitor center could not say for certain where those two rivers come together. Back home, some Colorado natives couldn't tell me where the Big Thompson met the Platte, although it was within three miles of their town; in Nebraska I found similar uncertainty as to the whereabouts of the various tributaries to the mighty Platte.

People do not seem so much concerned with where their rivers lead to as where they come from. Most mid-Nebraskans can tell you that the South Platte comes from Colorado, where a proposed dam called Two Forks threatens to reduce the flow of water to Nebraska farms. But can they tell you where the Republican River goes, after it leaves their state? Or where the Platte meets the Missouri?

Nebraska natives generally will tell you whether their family came from Germany, Czechoslovakia, England or Poland. The majority of westerners, in fact, can tell you about their family "headwaters": what country in Europe they came from, where they first settled, where they settled after that, and so on. But ask them where the *next* generation will settle, where the second and third generations down the line will be living, and they are at a loss to answer. They came from Ireland in 1742, had two generations in Pennsylvania, one in Kansas, one in Illinois, then one in South Dakota. But where are they headed? The question is, it seems, not worth a thought.

For a minute, before our bus entered the trees of timberline, back on Trail Ridge Road, I had a glimpse of the shining Colorado as it emerged from a forested canyon. Where had it come from? What did the headwaters look like? Is it possible, after all, to return to those sources, to find headwaters and ancestors, and to know them? In going against the current, backward in hydraulic time, you encounter just as many branchings as you would by going downstream. The problem is which to choose. Which would I rather do, go questing after indefinable beginnings or make a pilgrimage to the final destination of the river, somewhere on a dry delta near the sea?

Without really knowing it, I wanted to find something else at the headwaters of the Colorado River. I wanted to find some reassurance, somehow, that the headwaters will continue to nourish the flow. Without really meaning to, I found where that cataclysmic unleashing of the dammed-up river will begin.

With such vaguely defined motives in mind, one day in early August, a month after returning from my trip with the Colorado College students, I went looking for the source. I took my son, Rob, along. For the past few years, while he had been wandering in and out of various colleges in search of the right teacher, and on an odyssey to Puerto Rico looking for himself, I had been wandering and looking for confluences. Perhaps I had been looking for the perfect student. The idea of the two of us joining forces in a search for the headwaters seemed unusual at first, since we do not exactly step to the music of the same percussionists. This is, after all, the young man who came to his sister's formal wedding wearing argyle socks with a tuxedo. But then I saw a reason for having him along: perhaps, with luck, he could be the first man in history to have seen where the river begins *and*, years later, to see it rejoin the sea after all the engineering has collapsed. Not a very substantial probability, I admit, but at least he would enjoy the walk.

We camped above the upper end of Long Draw Reservoir, just at the northern edge of Rocky Mountain National Park, among knee-high alpine willow bushes. They have perfectly shaped, waxen, emerald-green leaves and polished maroon branches. They are stunted and tough; at 10,153 feet above the Sea of Cortez, willows cannot afford to be the wispy and wavy things that they are down lower, down where picnicking youth cut them for marshmallow sticks. The longest stick that you could find of the alpine willow would be so short that it would roast your knuckles along with your marshmallow. Crooked, too: they grow in low groves, huddling in a bit of moist soil, twining and bending to get their share of the thin sunshine, ducking under one another to avoid their share of the snowloads of winter. Underneath the thick canopy of bent branches and holly-green leaves there is a miniature environment of perpetual shade and moisture, where alpine birds and little mammals can live unseen.

Rob built the fire and put the ears of corn into the coals to cook and went for a hike before supper. I stayed behind, making notes so that I could remember what late afternoon is like, in August, up where the Colorado begins. While Rob was out there in the subalpine fir forest, out there in discovery meadows and goblin glens framed in deep green, the heavy-browed clouds pushed their ogre faces up over the stark bare granite ridges and watched over my shoulder while I stirred the chili and watched the coffee boil. The full clouds, too, churned and boiled. Rob made it back just in time; the chili was done and the corn was done, and the big drops of icy rain hissed in the fire and were dropping into our plates as we hustled under our shelter to eat. Dark dropped like a shawl of wet wool, fringed where it spanned the lower valley. The crags up the valley above us were not being rained on—at least not in any of the usual senses of "rain." Our mesa-gouging, granite-eating Colorado is not born from anything as common as mere "rain" such as you see filling the gutters of a city. At the Continental Divide, sharp cliffs rip open the bulging bellies of monstrous clouds and the water pours out, leaving the spent mass to sag down into the willow thickets.

Ordinarily, down where precipitation *does* take on ordinary forms, the dripping rain would last into the evening and through the night and would fall unnoticed behind the buildings. The rain would stay on the other side of doors in the dark and that would be that.

Before we had finished our supper, the storm moved off and the mountain daylight returned. Wounded clouds rose and pulled themselves loose from the peaks and floated away down the eastern slope like battered men-o'-war with their cumulus sails set for home. Brilliant blue sky became a dome over our valley. Sun made diamonds out of raindrops hanging on willow leaves and illuminated a thousand shiny hues of green: fir green and willow green, moss green and grass green, lichen green and algae green shone forth alongside malachite and aspen green.

And so *I* went for a walk. The low brush sprinkled me when I pushed through it, soaking cold through my pants. The late evening sun would last for perhaps a half-hour and then would be gone. When it is low and intense, the sunlight slanting through the valley shows tree-covered terraces running up the slopes. Perfectly regular shelves make an easy diagonal pattern of herringbone slopes—one-half of the herringbone on each side of the valley—visible only at this particular hour because the rays of the low sun are aligned with the tops of trees growing on glacial terraces. You would believe me if I said that a Japanese gardener had laid those terraces of alpine fir. But it was done by a glacier.

That sunshine! When it sits behind the mountains, up in this clear air, the sun's beams make the mountains look as though they have been cut out with a razor blade. When the sun shoots out a ray, that final ray of day, through a mountain gap at you . . . well, go and polish your largest brass tray and, when you can see your reflection in it, set it to throw full sunlight into your face. That's the sunset up on the Divide. Unbearable brightness, a fast series of color changes from brass to molten copper to burning sienna to silver-gold explosions to sudden dusk.

Walking in that same dusk, I came to a little stream of water, one I could easily jump across, that was flowing down from Specimen Mountain and that turned itself suddenly and, instead of flowing in the direction of Long Draw Reservoir, flowed burbling toward the west, toward the Pacific. Toward the Gulf of California, Sea of Cortez. I was looking along it down the Colorado River valley, and I was standing on the continent's dividing line, and this was the first tiny trickle of water going down the valley.

Stand here with me just a few minutes while the evening darkness deepens and I will describe How It All Begins, for it is a beginning that is perfectly in accord with this river's meanderings into and out of the affairs and the industries of man. It is in accord with its final destiny as an irrigation ditch for southern California.

Here is the valley. Stand at the Divide, facing downvalley. If you want, you can go right over there into the terraced forests and find a winking ribbon of water rippling down the mountain and going east. At your feet, a larger burble-run is busily heading west. But not always. Sometimes west, sometimes east, at the whim of man.

Off to our left, if we were to follow up this tiny watercourse, we would very soon realize that it is not a natural stream at all, but actually a ditch, a very old man-made ditch. We can see a long, high, massive mountain range extending clear out of sight along the south side of this deep valley; it is called Specimen Mountain, and many rivulets run down its time-riven slopes and through its lower forests; countless trickles escape from Specimen's icefields and snowpacks.

All the animals and most of the first humans to see all this escaping water were content to let it run down and become the Colorado River. They were not even curious, as I was, to find out which waters were the first to reach the valley floor and earn the name Colorado. Was it a wandering rivulet from the topmost icepack? Or was it a trickle that came out from under a rock and would hardly fill a canteen?

All of the animals and most of the men, I was saying, were content and uncurious—until some farmers came looking for more water than they had. It is not recorded to whom the Big Idea first occurred, but it is easy to see that he stood right here when it happened. Yessir. Look at all that irrigation going down the west slope and being wasted! Ain't no farming out there! The farms are all down the *east* slope, down in Greeley and Fort Morgan, Sterling and Burlington, Brush and Ault and Windsor! We need this water down there, and oh! if only there were a way to get it there. Not a tunnel—too expensive. But . . . well, well sure! It could be caught at timberline and diverted away from the Colorado drainage, turned to flow down the Poudre to the Platte. We, they agreed, could put all this rainfall and snowmelt into the Poudre River *right here!* The Poudre is more than just a mountain trout stream: it's a ready-made water delivery ditch!

So they formed a company and called it Larimer County Ditch Company and in 1881 or so they started cutting the Specimen Ditch. Men hacking rock with picks and moving rock in wheelbarrows, using pry bars to fracture and dislodge granite, obsidian, tufa, amalgam, and quartz by the ton, breathing hard at that elevation, slowly drove a ditch right across the face of Specimen Mountain. You can still see their work: you can hike for three miles or more through the forest corridor they cleared, along a dikelike stone barrier, wide enough at the top for a team and a Fresno scraper to pass, and right beside you is a ditch about four feet wide and so flat and smooth that the water in it looks like solid, transparent acrylic. You have to put your hand into it to see for yourself that it really *is* moving—you are surprised at how fast it is moving and how cold it is. It is so pure that you cannot tell how far up your wrist it comes.

This ditch. The men came up here each season, for perhaps three months if the weather held, and picked at the rock and piled up the dike. Many were Japanese teams, hired as companies; people speak of finding shards of broken rice bowls at the log cabin ruins at Ditch Camp Number One. The year 1884 arrived. Then 1885, 1886. Where's that water? the farmers asked. Finally, by 1890 it was flowing. Every drop of surface water coming down off Specimen Mountain for three lateral miles was stopped at the ditch, turned to flow eastward, and sent down to the beetfields and wheatfields and cornfields. And so the infant Colorado, its headwaters severed like neck arteries, still bleeds into eastern Colorado.

Grand Ditch was also being built in the 1880s. And it is grand, indeed. You can see it from your car when you cross Trail Ridge Road and look down the western slope: it's a long yellow slash across the mountains just below the timberline. From Trail Ridge Road, it looks like another road running across the far-off mountain.

No piker of a trench, this one. It is twenty feet wide and six feet deep, cut through solid rock and soft mud meadows, cut across a hundred watershed valleys high above the Colorado River (which was called the Grand River before being called the Colorado, you recall), cut for the one simple purpose of gathering up the Colorado River headwaters and forcing them to journey eastward rather than west-by-south.

Standing here where Specimen Ditch water hits a natural streambed and becomes the infant Poudre River, we can look down the Grand Valley and see Grand Ditch. Gray-granite gravel and sand, that beautiful glaciation-gray stone for a bottom; ice-clear water flowing so smoothly that you want to dash a stick or something into it to see how deep it really is and how it is moving; water making a soft chuckling talk against the sides of its confining ditch.

We could walk the ditch by taking the road that runs along its dike. Altogether we would walk fifteen miles to reach the end of it. Water started flowing down the trench in 1890, when it was much shorter; it was not finished to the fifteenth mile until 1936. If there had been a young man who hired himself in 1890 to dig that ditch, moving one stone at a time, two or three mountain months a year, laboring at ten thousand feet, he would no longer have been young when the crew reached the end of the line.

If we walk the whole fifteen miles, we will traverse the Never Summer Range. We will look down on the gold-rush ghost town of Lulu City. We will see the ditch arrest Bennett Creek, detain Lady Creek, capture Lulu Creek, drain all of Sawmill Creek, gather up the Little Dutch Creek and the Middle Dutch Creek and the Big Dutch; we will see where it gains the water flowing down Lost Creek—the ditch diggers reached there in 1911—and we'll pause where it cuts across and bleeds Mosquito Creek, then a few miles further around a mountain shoulder we will see Opposition Creek meet the opposition of the ditch dike. And when we get to Baker Creek we can quit, for that is where the ditch finally had to stop.

A little bit of water from some creeks, like Lady Creek and Lulu Creek, manages to seep through the ancient granite creviceways underneath the ditch and so continues its southeast-running journey. Downhill from Grand Ditch, Bennett Creek becomes a beautifully long waterfall hissing for eighty feet down a cliff face just before joining the Colorado River. Little springs and tiny seeps pop out below the ditch and run down to run west. Hundreds of nameless trickles. And, of course, on the opposite side of the valley and beyond the reach of Specimen Ditch, some of Specimen Mountain's waters still pour unhindered down to the westward-leading canyon. Tomorrow we will go that way and see that unhindered cascade. Perhaps it is the headwaters for which we seek. But for now the night is cold and the stars are out and it is time to call it a day.

That night, stretched out in my sleeping bag, I thought about the tides of Fall River. It was the river of my boyhood, the river I slept next to all through childhood and adolescence. Each night it sang me to sleep, and each morning it confirmed the new world. In winter it was quiet, hushed by snow. In the spring it roared and tumbled. And sometimes in the summer it had tides that I could not understand. From its headwaters to its confluence with the Thompson, Fall River is only thirteen miles long. How could it be over its banks one morning and a foot lower that evening?

Sometimes the drop of the river would awaken us, my brother and I. I suppose it was because we were always subconsciously aware of the noise the river made, and when it changed in the night we would wake up and wonder what had happened. I never did think much about it, really, until years later when an air force pilot told me a story about flying C-150s, huge four-engine cargo monsters. He had spent countless hours flying across the vast expanses of ocean between here and Japan. Sometimes the entire crew, except for the pilots, would go to sleep. When the time came to wake them up, he would make a very slight adjustment of one engine's throttle. That change in the tone of the engines, however subtle, would bring any drowsy aircrew to full and instant alert.

I knew that Fall River came from snowfields, and so when I was very young I reasoned that the level of the river rose and fell according to the rate of snowmelt. On a hot day, the snow would melt fast and cause a rise in the river the next morning. I had not been initiated yet, you see, into the facts of irrigation and electricity. Even though there were only ten miles of river between our house and those snowfield headwaters, and even though nine of those miles were inside the protection of Rocky Mountain National Park, there were dams on my river. A company, consisting of eight or ten farmers out at Greeley, owned a dam on Roaring Fork, which is a tributary of Fall River lying well inside the park. The second dam, hidden in a narrow canyon about a mile upstream from our house, ran a small power plant for the village of Estes Park.

I had seen these dams. I had seen every trickle of water in the valley. But to me they were only lakes. They were places to fish and to skip rocks, places for winter skating and sledding. Being too full of life and youthful energy ever to sit still, I was probably incapable of imagining that a running river—*my* river—could be detained and released at will. My river was the epitome of freedom to me. The words "Saturday" and "summer vacation" *meant* river. I knew it had its tides, its moments of rage and moments of flowing fullness; I also knew days when the current would almost cease altogether. But I had to become much older, in body and in spirit, before realizing what the tides meant.

~

But, to resume our narrative, nighttime took the mountains away and brought them back looking all shining and new the next morning, and we crawled from our beds to stand shivering like newly made men set naked in a newly made world. Coffee boiling had never smelled better. Granola and dried fruit with hot water poured over it had never been such a fine breakfast. The topographic map spread out on a rock had never looked so fascinating. We sipped the scalding coffee and danced away the cold and pointed shivering fingers at the wiggling lines on the map. Somewhere out there, we would find the headwater, the highest flow of water that could be the beginning of the Colorado River.

We struck out along Specimen Ditch, following the dike road as far as it went. When we came to the end of it, and the ditch, we decided that the snowfield dripping just above us was something of a start. It dribbled and drained into a mossy bank, which leaked and percolated into a scree slope, which sent an outpouring of collected water down through a heavily forested little canyon. I looked down into this dark cleft of the mountain. "What do you call this topographic feature?" I asked Rob, who held the map. "Perpendicular forest," he laughed.

And so, pausing only to agree never to tell his mother about this, we launched ourselves down through the perpendicular forest, determined to follow the course of this little creek to the bottom, to see whether it *met* the Colorado or *was* the Colorado. While it gleefully hurled itself over fallen logs, rushed headlong around boulders, paused and then purled right over a pile of moraine-deposited rubble, we slid and slipped from handhold to handhold, from fir branch to aspen sapling; or we squished through spring-fed and snow-fed marshes of muck; or we balanced along logs and squeezed past the trees on game trails; and we followed the creek down. And down.

The small stream slid almost silently through a soggy green bog, a place so overgrown with mosses and bushes that it seemed to be a scene from some fantasy about trolls or leprechauns. A huge and ancient tree had toppled here, many years ago, and what was left of it was a mossy mound like a miniature mountain, full of caves and overhangs and distorted green shapes. We plodded and ploughed through the sucking sod and came to a place that was as dry as this one was wet. It was an avalanche area, a narrow defile on the side of the mountain where the stream had cut through loose, dry, yellow scree. Here and there a stunted pine clung to the pitch of the slope, but otherwise the gorge was devoid of trees and brush.

At first we tried to traverse the loose gravel slope, but when each step we took started an avalanche of rocks and dirt, we decided that the stream could be followed from the top of the ridge. We would not see as much of it, but at least we wouldn't be buried beside it. Rob and I stepped carefully, cautiously, even in the comparatively stable ground along the ridgeline. The stream, however, poured right on through this place without slowing; looming above it were acres of bare, loose rock barely plastered in place with crumbling dry mountain soil. The mountain angle seemed to defy gravity. The whole mountainside had obviously slid down there and was just as obviously ready to do it again at a moment's footfall.

We came at last to a granite cliff. It was dense, hard rock: the roiling water had eroded away the loose earth quickly, but it would need a few thousand more years to dissolve the stone. Our creek now took a final leap over the edge, crashed onto the slope below, and found itself at the bottom of the valley. The top of Grand Valley. Clinging to aspens and spruce branches and chokecherry bushes, we also went over the granite shelf and arrived upon the banks of the infant Colorado River. We looked back up at the precipitous perpendicular forest above, and then looked down at our feet. Our headwater river was being met by another flow, a flow just as large, coming from somewhere up the valley. This was not the source, but only a confluence.

I was not concerned or disappointed, however; I was too preoccupied with the scene that the area presented to us. I was caught up in a wonderful comparison—an irony, if you will. Far, far down the Colorado, where I had ridden in a rubber boat, the river has carved the rock into a garden of sculpted shapes. And here at the headwaters, where you would expect to find some sodden tundra slowly releasing moisture like an overburdened sponge, where you would expect to find hard granite crevices for the streambed, lined with stately spruce and fir, the thin trickle had also been carving out phantasmagoria. The river of Canyonlands, the creator of the Grand Canyon, begins its downward run in one of the Rocky Mountains' most unusual and scenic headwaters, a place appropriately known as the Little Yellowstone.

To understand how all these soft yellow-rock shapes came to be here, contained by a border of thick gray granite, we need to look at some background, if you'll pardon the pun, of Specimen Mountain. The first geologists who became aware of this rather unusual lump in the Rocky Mountain chain assumed that it was an ancient volcano. This is a natural assumption to make, because on slopes that lie above timberline where the wind and storms expose the soil, and in the eroded valleys, you find layers of rhyolite on top of layers of hardened ashflow, which in turn sit atop layers of mudflow rock containing hunks of obsidian and several lesser species of volcanic spew. It is called "Specimen" Mountain, presumably, because so many specimens of different volcanic-associated minerals can be found there.

In the 1960s, a geologist named R. B. Taylor took a considerably closer look at this "volcano." Something bothered him about it. The big cirque, always assumed to be an eroded crater, didn't seem big enough or deep enough to have ejected all that material. More curious, however, was that the volcano—if it had been a volcano—had somehow done something unheard of: it had managed to explode in such a way as to have all of its volcanic garbage come to rest on *top* of itself. In other words, everything ejected had to have gone straight up and then straight down again. This struck Taylor as very odd behavior, since a volcano usually blows its magma and other junk far away from its core. There didn't even seem to *be* a core, in fact; this whole mountain seemed to be made of debris.

Some miles away from Specimen Mountain there is an unmistakable volcano; at an estimated age of 28 million years, it is fairly young compared with the uplift holocaust that sent the Rockies crashing up. It is

Lulu Mountain. Geologist Taylor's theory is that when Lulu heaved up her molten ash, her molten obsidian, her boiling mud-lava flows, it all came pouring down through a deep granite trench, oozing its red-hot length along for eight or ten miles until it cooled and piled up in a long, massive, yellow mountain that people would call Specimen. There would be the obsidian, chunks of it glowing in the liquid rock mud; there would be the thick cloud of yellow ash rising, hovering for weeks, falling into thicker and thicker layers.

Neither Taylor nor I was there at the time. But at the foot of Specimen Mountain on the north side, where the Colorado River is only about a foot wider than a long-legged boy can conveniently jump, the rock is soft and yellow stuff, like petrified ashes from a furnace (for those who can remember furnaces that produced yellow smelly ash). In this rock are specks of black glass: obsidian. In it are also vacant holes: tufa, mudflow, bubbles of gas preserved by the cooling of molten rock. What is *not* in it is much granite, the primary rock of the Rockies. So the crumblestone is yellowish and consistent in texture. In the cliff face opposite the point where our little kamikaze creek enters, you can see sediment layers in the stone, uplifted to a forty-five-degree angle. But other than that single bit of visual variation, the valley walls have absolute unbroken color and texture, like jaundiced plaster.

Okay. That is the terrain. Sitting almost at the Continental Divide, a massive block of soft yellow stone. *Now* picture this: titanic storms come surging and staggering up the prehistoric, barren, steaming slopes from the west or from the east, and they rage and rip and howl over the summit line of the continent. A year of cumulus clouds being broken open and spilled on the range of mountains. A rainstorm every day for a hundred years— 36,500 storms. A thousand years pass, and then a thousand more. In those thousands, how often does the concussion of hard thunder slam down on the exposed stone? How many thousands of times do we see lightning come zigzagging down and hissing, cracking into the rock? And always there is the rain. Rain in patient, persistent, unending drizzle. Rain in masculine downthrusts. Rain driven anglewise by extreme winds. The Earth globe tilts into its axis, and the rain becomes sleet and ice, ice and sleet, melting and running into cracks, invading the vacant gas-holes and freezing there and expanding. Grain by grain, one bit of sand at a time or a hundred tons in one avalanche, without the witness of a single living thing even remotely resembling man, the weather patiently removes the mountain of volcanic detritus.

What did twenty million years of weather leave behind, in the Little Yellowstone valley? Not plain polished granite such as you find in most canyons out here, or cloven and shattered cliffs such as those that are the walls of the Big Thompson Narrows. Here, it left tall ocher spires and open hallways between knife-blade-like hogbacks. It left stone formations that look like cleavers holding their edges up to the sky. It left castle turrets and skinny domes, and fragile-looking termite mounds two hundred feet high, and yellow monoliths whose hawklike faces look down along the Colorado's Grand Valley.

The ground here seems almost sterile, like fresh ash. It is loose gravel, loose scree, loose sand, loose silt. The infant Colorado River runs along through this strange soil, moving it aside or taking it further downstream. The water runs clear, and the rocks under the water look even more yellow than those that remain dry. Out in the farming country fed by the redirected river, we would see this as shameful erosion, a tragic waste of soil. Up here on the roof of the Rockies, it seems natural and at the same time almost grotesque.

Robert jumps the Colorado River and goes scrambling, alone, up one of the unstable-looking yellow fins of rock. When he is up high enough to be in some danger, I get out my telephoto lens and take his picture so that his mother will have something to remember him by. When he returns, he tries to finesse his way around my displeased scowl by awakening my professorial superiority. "So, Dad," he opens, "what do you think caused all these incredible rock formations?" "Poor range management," I reply, and we laugh.

Little Yellowstone is, as advertised, a little valley of yellow rock formations. Some look amusingly like inverted ice cream cones; others resemble massive shark fins so much that you think you could dig down at the base of them and find the whole fossilized form of the prehistoric fish itself. Here the juvenile Colorado practices her first attempts at stone-sculpting, constantly cutting and carving and eroding and excavating. She seems to be playing with the soft stone, practicing random and wayward shapes. A few miles below us, down in Phantom Valley and well into the thick timber and level moraines, she becomes a young lady on an outing, purring and meandering through nice mud meadows, stroking the sides of pet trout. Down there, our debutante river will move the willow curtains aside and step onto flowered, aspen-trimmed stages to sing her soft ripple songs. But up here at the foot of Specimen, where she is still finding herself, she carves away at the mountain like a kid turned loose with a shiny new shovel.

The afternoon grew older and the spruce shade stretched out toward the east, and we left the valley. Rob and I climbed (and the word is *climbed*) up out of the Little Yellowstone, shunning the trail, and found the Grand Ditch and walked back toward camp, still stopping to look back down into the chasm, stopping to examine tiny rivulets that flow from the ditch downward toward the larger stream, and we asked ourselves over and over whether we had found the headwaters.

In that we found the highest drainage of the Colorado River, yes. This place is the headwater. What we could not do is to seek out the tiniest, highest trickle of that drainage and trace it uphill until we could be certain that . . . there! *that* particular drop of water just now falling from the melting edge of the snowpack at thirteen thousand feet above sea level, *that* is the first birth of the Colorado! . . . no.

There are rivers in the world that begin when they emerge from the ground as a bubbling spring, or flow out of a lake, and therefore have easily identified origins. But the source of the Colorado is a gestalt kind of thing. The whole of it, in that high valley, is more than the sum of the tributaries. What we found was the birthplace of a river's spirit. The headwater is a valley and the range of a mountain. It is shaped like a leaf with many veins, Thoreau's basic pattern for God's organic systems. It's shaped like a hand with ten thousand acres held between its valley-fingers; the veins come down, the arteries come down, the lifeblood comes down and down and finally comes to a place where it can be named, although it can never be fully known.

In the long run of things, it will not matter that Specimen Ditch and Grand Ditch ever interrupted the Colorado River here at the head valleys, any more than it will matter that the great dams temporarily impeded its flow through the steep desert canyons. Someday, a prize-size elk will come running downhill and stumble and drown in Specimen Ditch while the ditch is running summer-full, and its body will dam it and cause a washout in the dike wall. Being almost level, the water in the ditch will run backward and come to the end of the dike and then plummet down through the perpendicular forest to the Colorado. Rob knows what I mean: he has hazarded that hill and knows how a downhill-racing elk could trip and die in the ditch, and how the ditch could erode its sides and run backward through the breach, and how a freezing heavy rain could keep the ditch-rider in his cabin long enough for the water to undo the work of the laborers.

As for Grand Ditch, there will come an unusually slow-moving and unusually heavy storm. We call them "hundred-year storms," because a hundred years seems like an impressive span of time to us. Like its prehistoric predecessors, this storm will spend days drowning the whole Big Dutch drainage and inundating the Middle Dutch and the Mosquito. And when all of that overflow of life's fluid suddenly hits the Grand Ditch, it will *not* just turn like a docile demoiselle and go meekly to irrigate some flatland beetfield; instead, on this particular storm day, it will go straight on over the ditch dike. It will run down to join the Colorado in a trip toward Baja.

It will take that section of the ditch down the hill with it and leave the dirt in the Little Yellowstone Valley. An Eaton beet farmer subscribing to the irrigation company will be asked to help pay for some repairs. He'll put a spoonful of Hawaii cane sugar into his coffee, look out at his pivot irrigation system sucking up the Ogalala Aquifer to spray over his corn crop, and he will reply, "I guess not."

So. The Colorado begins up here, here where we stand in the last light of a short day. Here it seems almost indifferent to man's petty thefts of its moisture for his sugar beets; none of its soul or spirit has been touched. It's still there. I was glad to discover that. It's elusive, but still there. Robert even sensed the river's spirit and mystery as we stood there looking, staring into the crystal-clear ditch water. For no reason that we could see, there were transparent oval shapes in the stream. They moved along like disks of clear oil in the water, distortions against the gravel bottom. It looked like hundreds of thin plastic lenses had been dropped there and were floating along the bottom. The water was otherwise invisible. "Watershadows" Rob decided to name these little mystery shapes.

"Watershadow," I repeated. "That would be a good name for a canoe."

"It's a metaphor," he said.

"Thanks," I said. "I know that."

Envoi

Roused from naptime dreams of
    Milk and cookies,
The sit-upon rugs rolled up and
    All put away,
It was time for them to act out a story.

Moving among diminutive divas
    And baby Barrymores
I came to a small boy standing quietly alone,
    Waiting to begin his part in "The Story of Ferdinand."

"You must be Ferdinand," I offered,
    "You are very good at standing still."
"I'm one of the flowers," he sniffled,
    "But I could be Ferdinand. If I wanted to."

Sometimes it's hard to be a flower,
    Wondering what it would be like
To be the one who picks the flowers instead.

But if you were a flower—a meadow daisy or briar rose,
    Let us say—
Could you imagine being anything else?

About the Author

James C. Work is Professor Emeritus from Colorado State University. He holds a doctorate in Victorian Poetry and Victorian Studies, and is the author of ten books, including westerns and mysteries. Western American literature first heard of Work in 1984 when he took on the job of restoring Jack Schaefer's novel *Shane* for the University of Nebraska Press. Since then he has published *Prose and Poetry of the American West,* an anthology that won the Colorado Seminars in Literature Annual Book Award. He also wrote *Following Where the River Begins,* which is included here in its entirety, and it won the Charles Redd Award in Western Studies. He was also the editor of a collection of short stories titled *Gunfight!* that includes many stories by western favorites. He lives in Colorado.